Megabyte

Simon Cotton, Graham Teager, Rob Austin

OXFORD

OXFORD
UNIVERSITY PRESS

Great Clarendon Street, Oxford OX2 6DP

Oxford University Press is a department of the University of Oxford.
It furthers the University's objective of excellence in research,
scholarship, and education by publishing worldwide in

Oxford   New York

Auckland Cape Town Dar es Salaam Hong Kong Karachi
Kuala Lumpur Madrid Melbourne Mexico City Nairobi
New Delhi Shanghai Taipei Toronto

With offices in
Argentina Austria Brazil Chile Czech Republic France Greece
Guatemala Hungary Italy Japan Poland Portugal Singapore
South Korea Switzerland Thailand Turkey Ukraine Vietnam

Oxford is a registered trade mark of Oxford University Press
in the UK and in certain other countries © Oxford University Press 2002

The moral rights of the authors have been asserted

Database right Oxford University Press (maker)

This edition first published 2002

British Library Cataloguing in Publication Data

Data available

ISBN: 978 0 19 832825 4

20 19 18 17 16 15 14 13 12 11 10

Typeset in Palatino, Bulldog and Imperfect

Printed in China by Printplus

*Oxford University Press accepts no responsibility for
material published on websites referred to in this book.*

*Website addresses included were correct at time of
going to press, but be aware that these may change.*

*Paper used in the production of this book is a natural,
recyclable product made from wood grown in sustainable forests.
The manufacturing process conforms to the environmental
regulations of the country of origin.*

Acknowledgments

We would like to thank the following organisations for
their contributions to this book:
The Met. Office, Ford, The Police Force, Tesco's plc,
Trinity House Lighthouses

The Publisher would like to thank the following for
permission to reproduce photographs:
Allsport: p 54 (bottom); AMD: p 8 (bottom); Arun Electronics:
p 131; Camera Press: p 54 (middle); Corbis UK Ltd/Julie
Houke: p 16 (bottom); Corbis UK Ltd/Wolfgang Kaehler:
p 163Corbis UK Ltd/Neil Rabinowitz: p 22 (top); Corbis
Stockmarket/Alexandra Steedman: p 108; Corel Professional
Photos: pp 25, 93 (bottom), 127 (top); Cities Revealed/The
GeoInformation Group, 2001 and Crown Copyright: p 29;
Digital Vision: pp 30, 41, 43, 48 (bottom), 93 (top);
Economatics: p 130; Ford Motor Company Ltd: p 32; FPG
International: p 75; Hulton Getty: p 16 (top); IBVA
Technologies/Drew Delitto: 15 (middle); The Image Bank:
pp 21, 52 (left), 110, 134; Intel: p 8 (middle); Jaguar Cars Ltd:
pp 33, 126; The Met Office/Crown Copyright: pp 60, 61
(bottom), 62 (bottom; The Met Office/P Gavin: p 62 (top);
The Met Office/I MacGregor: p 61 (top); Mirror Syndication
International: p 53 (top); Newsteam/Cadbury World: pp 26, 28
(top); Oxford University Press: pp 8 (top), 16 (middle), 36, 38,
51 (bottom), 123, 125 (top), 127 (bottom), 169 (all); Oxford
University Press/Mark Mason: pp34, 37: Photodisc: pp 12, 50
(bottom), 93 (middle), 125 (bottom); Press Association: p 15
(left), Nick Reed: p 56; Geoff Rushbrook: p 10 (bottom);
Science Photo Library: pp10 (bottom), 59 (bottom); Science
Photo Library/Adam Hart-Davis: pp 10 (top), 64, : Science
Photo Library/Ken E Johns: p 51 (top); Science Photo
Library/James King-Holmes: pp 28 (bottom), 128 (right);
Science Photo Library/Maximilian Stock Ltd: pp 27, 31;
Science Photo Museum/Sam Ogden: p 128 (left); Science Photo
Library/David Parker: p 68: Science Photo Library/Philippe
Plailly/Eurelios: p 15 (right), Science Photo Library/Volker
Steger: pp 59 (top), 66; Science Photo Library/Weiss/Jerrican:
p 124; Stone: pp 5, 22 (bottom), 39, 46, 157, 173; Telegraph
Colour Library: p 52 (right); Thames Valley Police: p 67;
Trinity House: pp 48 (right), 50 (top); Waitrose Ltd: p 35.

Illustrations are by Richard Anderson, Martin Aston, Stefan
Chabluk and David Russell.

With special thanks to Tesco Stores, Cowley, Oxford.

Contents

Preface

Section A ICT in our lives

Section B ICT skills

Section C National curriculum projects

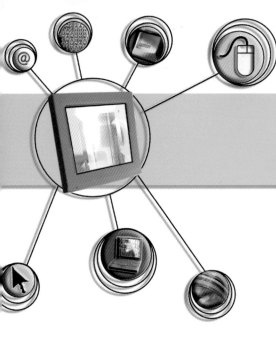

Preface

Key to symbols used in Sections A and B

 Unit objectives

 Navigation symbol

 Desk task

 Computer task

 Computer instructions

Megabyte is for students following the ICT Key Stage 3 National Curriculum and related programmes of study. The materials have all been trialled with mixed ability groups of Key Stage 3 students in two mixed comprehensive schools.

The materials in *Megabyte* are presented in three sections, to give teachers maximum flexibility in how they use them.

Section A presents ICT in a variety of contexts, providing a firm foundation for later project work. Each unit contains desk tasks and computer tasks, to help the teacher in planning lessons where there are not enough computers for the whole class to use at one time.

Section B provides skills-based chapters, for use as instructional guides or for reference. Skills covered range from basic word processing to DTP, creating web pages and designing control systems.

In Sections A and B navigation symbols (see left) highlight links between units, and between skills and context, helping students to understand how to approach tasks as well as what content they should strive to use in a piece of work.

Section C contains 15 projects, each providing a context for one of the national curriculum units as set out by QCA. In some cases the project topics are intentionally different from those suggested by QCA, to encourage innovation and foster students' interests. The projects may be used either at the end of a unit, or as a part of the teaching for the unit. Suitable for students across the ability range, they offer students the opportunity to show their understanding of ICT use in the contexts in Section A, as well as to demonstrate their ICT skills.

The website linked to this book may also be helpful for further investigation and study: www.oup.com/uk/megabyte.

Simon Cotton
Graham Teager
Rob Austin

ICT in our lives

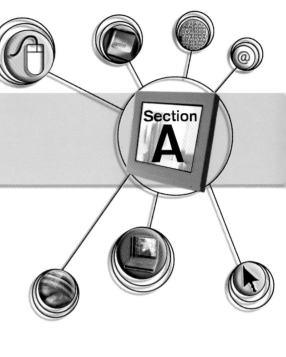

Information and Communications Technology (ICT) equipment is now used to perform many tasks that affect our daily lives. Without it the world would be a very different place.

1 The world about us

Information and Communications Technology (ICT) affects every aspect of our lives – in our homes, on a journey, and in shops and banks. At school and at work ICT makes our lives easier. ICT can model, control and monitor processes, for example in factories. ICT allows us to gather information from all over the world in an instant and to present that information in suitable ways for different audiences and for different purposes.

In this unit you will:

- get a basic understanding of what ICT means
- see how ICT affects our lives
- learn about the components of a personal computer.

ICT in daily life

1 List three examples where ICT is used to:

- **present** information
- **gather** information
- **control** machines/devices
- **model** situations.

2 From the picture give three examples of how ICT makes our lives easier.

3 List three ways in which ICT is used in your school.

4 Think about a visit to the Bank or Post Office. Describe all the ways that ICT is used there.

5 Has ICT been good for all sections of the community? Give an example of someone who may not benefit from ICT and explain why.

ICT and the personal computer

There are **three** types of personal computer (PC) in common use.

1 Desk-top: designed to be used at home or in the office in one place. Desk-tops are often linked together or networked to share software and data. Each PC is then called a workstation.

2 Notebook or laptop: small, light and with built-in screen, mouse, speakers, microphone and modem. It has a rechargeable battery.

3 Palmtop: extremely small, designed to be carried in a pocket and used anywhere.

Palmtops allow you to work on the move. Data can be transferred later to a PC.

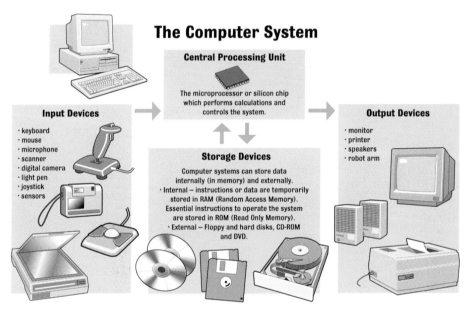

The Computer System

Central Processing Unit

The microprocessor or silicon chip which performs calculations and controls the system.

Input Devices
· keyboard
· mouse
· microphone
· scanner
· digital camera
· light pen
· joystick
· sensors

Storage Devices

Computer systems can store data internally (in memory) and externally.
· Internal – instructions or data are temporarily stored in RAM (Random Access Memory). Essential instructions to operate the system are stored in ROM (Read Only Memory).
· External – Floppy and hard disks, CD-ROM and DVD.

Output Devices
· monitor
· printer
· speakers
· robot arm

How PCs operate

Any **computer system** allows you to enter data, process data, store data and then output the results.

At the heart of the PC is the central processing unit (CPU). This is a single microprocessor or silicon chip. It performs all the calculations needed for the computer to work. The complicated CPU circuits are printed on to the silicon chip using a photographic process. The chip is fitted on to a printed circuit board contained in the main box of the computer.

Hardware

Any device attached or built into the main box is called a peripheral.

Peripherals used to put data into the computer are called input devices, e.g. keyboard, scanner.

Peripherals used to present data from the computer are called output devices, e.g. monitor or visual display unit (VDU), printer.

Two types of CPU.

The main box and the peripherals are the hardware. For the computer to operate it must have software loaded. This is a series of instructions known as a program that tell the computer what to do.

Operating systems

Every PC needs an **operating system**. This is the software that:

- operates the peripheral devices

- decides in what order the PC should carry out tasks

- provides a standard visual display on the monitor when no applications software is running.

Some examples of operating systems used on PCs are:

- the Windows operating systems Windows 95, 98, 2000

- IBM systems OS/2 and Warp.

Windows Operating systems are the most popular systems around the world.

Software

Applications software or programs allow you to perform different tasks on the PC. Applications software includes word processors, spreadsheets, data handling, desktop publishing (DTP) and graphics packages.

Introducing file types

Each piece of software used with computer hardware is made up of files. A file is a collection of related data. Some files you create yourself, and other files are created by software designers. All these files contain code or instructions for the computer to read.

You can tell a lot about files by their file name extensions. A file name extension always follows the dot after the file name.

Here are some of the most common file name extensions:

File name extension	Type
.doc .txt	Word processing document
.jpg .gif .bmp	Files containing image data
.exe	Files containing code

For example, if you want to load *Word*, you need the Winword.exe file. The extension .exe tells you this is a program file. If you are looking for an image file, you know that it will not be one of the files ending in .doc or .txt.

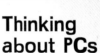

Thinking about PCs

1 Draw and label your own diagram of a Personal Computer System.

2 Copy the table headings.

Input device	Output device

List all the peripherals you can under the correct headings.

3 Are there any peripherals that can be used both to input and to output data?

FACT FILE

1 The first computers

The first digital computer was designed by the British inventor Charles Babbage. The Science Museum in London has recently constructed one of his designs.

2 Bits

The term bit is short for 'binary digit'. One bit represents either 0 or 1 in the binary number system and is the smallest unit of information that can be handled by a computer. It takes eight bits to write a single letter or number. This string of eight bits is called a byte.

3 Bytes

A byte is so small that computer memory is measured in kilobytes (kb), megabytes (Mb) and gigabytes (Gb).

1 Mb = 1024 kb

1 Gb = 1024 Mb

4 Qwerty keyboards

The keys on the keyboard are usually arranged so that the top row of letters spells out QWERTY, which gives it the name qwerty keyboard. This keyboard layout is the same as for old-fashioned mechanical typewriters. The arrangement of letters was designed so that the most frequently used letters were spread out over the keyboard. This helped to stop the typewriter's mechanical levers jamming when you were typing fast.

5 Pixels

The smallest rectangular element that a VDU can display is called a pixel. All the letters, numbers and pictures that you see on the VDU are made up of coloured pixels. The clarity or level of detail that you can see depends upon how many pixels are being used. This is known as the resolution.

The computer stores information about each pixel in an image, so that it can create the image again. For black and white images, the information for each pixel is either 'black' or 'white' and so the encoding for each pixel can be stored in one bit. For this reason the graphical image created using this technique is called a 'bit map'.

For more complex images the information about each pixel needs more than one bit of storage, but the name 'bit map' is still used. Image files with the extensions .bmp, .gif and .jpg are all created by the bit map technique.

A typical screen resolution is 640 pixels across by 480 pixels down. This is called Video Graphics Array.

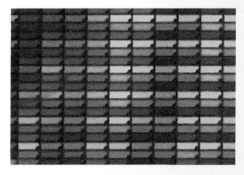

Colour on a VDU is produced by red, green and blue pixels.

Humanities day trip

1 Your humanities tutor is arranging a visit to a local medieval castle. Complete the following table to help your teacher select the most appropriate applications software for different parts of the planning.

TASK	SUGGESTED SOFTWARE	PROGRAM TYPE
Letter home explaining visit and asking for permission	Microsoft® *Word* or *Word Perfect*	
Poster for tutor base advertising visit and reminding students to take letter home		
Table of emergency telephone numbers for students attending visit		Data handling program
Method of calculating cost per student		
Presentation, including pictures, of fortifications seen on visit	Microsoft® *Powerpoint*	

Now design and create the poster for the visit.

Don't forget to think about your target audience. How will you attract their attention?

2 Match these file name extensions to their descriptions:

.jpg .exe .htm .txt .rtf .xls .wav .csv .bmp .gif

	An extension that shows that a file can be executed or loaded by entering the filename at the DOS prompt, or by double clicking on it in *Windows*.
22	A file whose contents are instructions for a **web page**.
21	The second most popular image format used on the internet.
19	A **sound file** (hint: sound travels in waves).
	A simple text file, which does not record the information about alignment and other commands that affect how the text is displayed on the page.
	A file from an *Excel* spreadsheet.
	A text file in rich text format. This allows the information about document layout and different type styles to be transferred to other software.
21	The standard format for reducing the size of **image files**. The main type of image file used on the internet.
15	A file format used to transfer information between **databases** or between a database and other software. Called a comma separated values file (csv), because each record is displayed on one line, with commas separating the fields.
	A bitmap graphics file. This does not compress the information about the image. It is not often used on the internet as it takes a long time to download or view these files.

Hardware and software

1 Design a poster advertising a second-hand PC for sale. Think about your target audience.

a How will you attract their attention?

b What technical information do you think they need about this PC?

2 Homes of the future

In this unit you will:

- learn how computers are being developed to make our lives easier
- consider the problems and benefits of the modern computerised home.

The homes of the future will be very different from our homes today. Some of the jobs currently done by humans will be taken over by computers, which should make people's lives much easier.

We already have some of the basic technology for the homes of the future. But the digital televisions, intelligent refrigerators and advanced computer technology of the future will be very different from the products we have today. As technology develops, voice and handwriting recognition as well as robotic control will become a more important part of their design.

Our great-grandparents could not have imagined the everyday items we now take for granted – telephones, television, the internet, fridge-freezers. So we cannot know exactly what homes will be like in the future. But we can predict that the house control computer will become a central part of day-to-day living.

Computer control

In the future home, all the household systems could be controlled by a central computer. This computer will ensure energy is used efficiently, for example by controlling heating levels and turning off lights when a room is empty. It will also manage security when the owner is away from the home. By taking over a range of tasks, which will save time and make the living environment more pleasant, the computer will make life more relaxing for the home's occupants.

10
18
The central computer will rely on **sensors** for its operation. By **monitoring** the conditions of the house, including heating and lighting, it will be able to ensure that things are functioning exactly to the owner's instructions.

Look at the picture of the house of the future. In this house motion sensors constantly monitor movement in all the rooms. At night when all the occupants of the house are in bed these sensors are used by the security system. In the day the sensors monitor the movements of the occupants around the house, ensuring that the daily cleaning of the house by robotic cleaners does not interfere with the owners' use of the house. Just imagine what living in a futuristic house might be like.

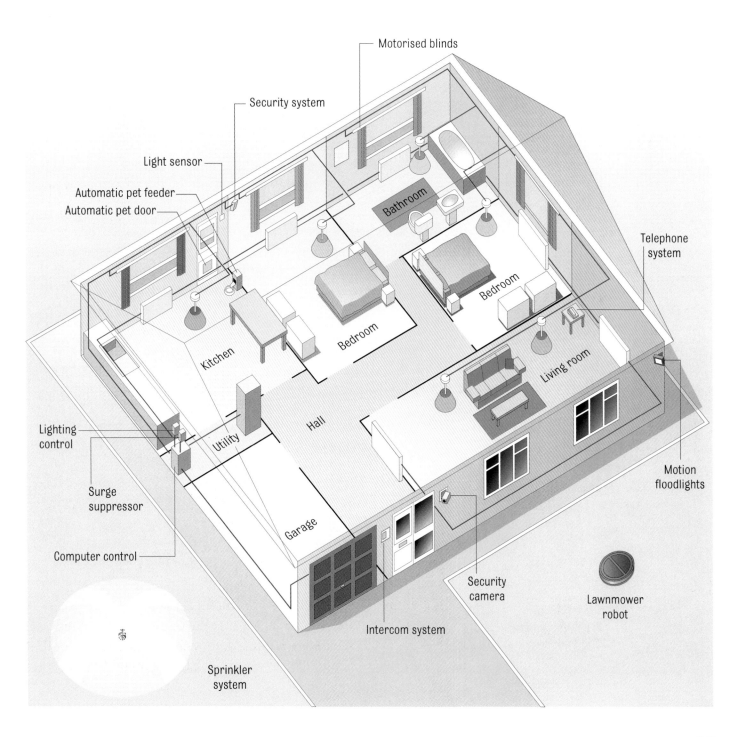

Motorised blinds

Security system

Light sensor

Automatic pet feeder

Automatic pet door

Bathroom

Telephone system

Bedroom

Bedroom

Kitchen

Living room

Lighting control

Hall

Utility

Surge suppressor

Motion floodlights

Computer control

Garage

Security camera

Lawnmower robot

Intercom system

Sprinkler system

The advantages of computer control

People living in homes of the future will enjoy the benefits of this computer control but may find it causes some problems too.

18 Because the house is **controlled** by a central computer, the home will make the most efficient use of energy possible. Energy costs will be reduced as lighting, heating, audio systems, etc. will only be operational when rooms are in use. Telephone bills will be reduced as the central computer chooses the cheapest tariff available for each 'phone call. Refrigerators will issue warnings when food products are out of date and will shop around using the internet to get the best deal possible from supermarkets.

The computer-controlled home will also allow disabled or elderly people to have a more comfortable lifestyle. Tasks such as filling and operating the kettle, turning on taps and cutting the grass can be difficult for people in wheelchairs or with poor hand control. If the home-owner cannot operate a computer keyboard, voice recognition software will allow them to activate things in the home simply by giving instructions.

But these systems are not without problems. In particular they rely on electricity to function and on the correct operation of the central computer system. In a power cut, or if there is a failure in the central computer, the house could become a very cold, dark and lonely place.

A typical start to a day in the future

Helen is a Public Relations Officer for a large company. Her day typically starts at 6.00 a.m. As the sun rises the curtains open automatically, letting light into the bedroom. Lighting and heating conditions are checked and the information fed back to the central computer. Before Helen gets up the central computer adjusts the heating and lighting so that the levels are just as she has programmed them.

Before Helen leaves the house she collects buttered toast and a cup of tea already prepared for her by machines in the kitchen. The refrigerator has automatically ordered a delivery of goods via the internet, including more butter.

As Helen enters the garage the lights come on and the main door opens for her. The lawnmower and sprinkler systems activate to work on her garden. Everything is protected from theft by security detection and surveillance systems, which she can check on from her office via the internet.

While she is at work Helen remembers she has friends coming round that evening. Using the internet she instructs the central computer to admit her guests if she does not arrive home in time. She also checks the contents of the fridge to make sure she has something for dinner. Her working day can now begin.

1 Sensors help the central computer obtain information about the conditions in the house. What sensors might be in operation in Helen's house?

2 Helen made use of the internet in her home. How do you think the following organisations could make the most use of the internet in the future?

- Hospitals
- Television companies
- Schools
- Record companies

Gadgets of the future

Perhaps home-owners of the future will have useful gadgets like these:

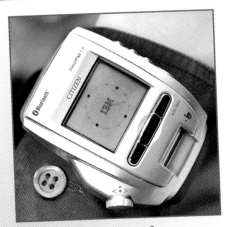

Never lose track of your activities again!

This new development in wristwatch technology keeps your diary, controls the television, stereo and video and of course keeps the time. Programmable functions enable it to remind you of birthdays, anniversaries and appointments. And to keep in touch on the move, use its mobile phone feature.

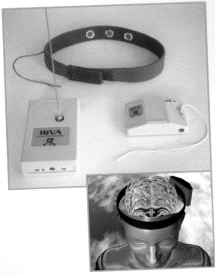

Communicate with your computer
simply through the power of thought. Write, drive, play games or music, all through this revolutionary neural interface.

With these handy robots,
mowing the lawn or sweeping the floor will never be a chore again! While you are out these useful appliances make sure your house and garden are clean and tidy.

Infamous quotes

In the past, computers were not seen as a useful part of the future.

"Computers in the future may have only 1000 vacuum tubes and perhaps only weigh $1\frac{1}{2}$ tons."

Popular Mechanics, 1949

In 1949 a single computer filled a whole building

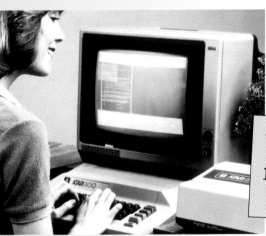

"There is no reason for any individual to have a computer in their home."

Ken Olson (President of Digital Equipment Corporation), 1977

"640k ought to be enough for anybody."

Bill Gates (Founder and CEO of Microsoft), 1981

Modern PCs are about 64 000 000k = 64Mb

"I think there is a world market for about five computers."

Thomas J. Watson (Chairman of the Board of IBM), 1943

In 2001 there were about 200 million personal computers worldwide.

Computers in control

1 Think of 10 tasks a computer may undertake in a home of the future.

Write your ideas in a table with these headings:

Important tasks	Essential tasks	Non-essential tasks

2 Now consider the same list of tasks for a disabled or elderly person in a home of the future.

Explain each task in detail, explaining if any of the tasks change category in this case.

3 What do you think could happen if the following parts of your future home failed or malfunctioned?

- The main electricity supply.
- The main computer control unit.
- The computer connection to the lighting system.
- The temperature control system.
- Cooker or electric heating controls.

4 How could you prevent failure of the critical systems in a future home?

5 Do you think a computer-controlled home would be an improvement on homes today?

The homes of the future

Choose **one** of the following activities.

Think carefully about the package you use to complete the task.

1 You are the editor of a national magazine. Write a response to a campaigner who has written to you claiming that the futuristic home will make people lazy.

Explain the benefits and drawbacks of such a house in your response, which will be printed in next month's edition.

2 Draw a house of the future. Either use a drawing package to create your own house of the future or draw your plan freehand and use a scanner to acquire the picture.

Label each feature on your plan or picture and write a short explanation of each task the computer will help you perform.

3 Create a poster to advertise an exhibition of your house of the future or a product of the future.

Your poster must include:

- date
- time
- place
- contact name and number
- a brief description of the event
- a catchy slogan
- a rough cartoon or other picture of the house/product of the future.
- entrance cost
- details of workshops you can attend.

    For example: 'Visit our curtain control workshops. We promise you'll never have to close your curtains again.'

The airport

ICT equipment is used in every aspect of airport management. Every day ICT systems are used to ensure that thousands of passengers get on the right planes, and that their luggage goes with them.

Behind the scenes ICT systems ensure the smooth running in four main areas:

1 The terminal building
2 Commercial systems
3 Airport information systems
4 Flight planning and control

In this unit you will:

- look at how ICT is used in airport management and operation
- find out how ICT is used in air traffic control.

Terminal building

ARRIVALS

Baggage and cargo

Air traffic control

Baggage and cargo

1 Terminal building

This is the part of the airport that the public sees. Thousands of passengers pass through the terminal building each day. They use credit cards and loyalty cards, and take advantage of special flight deals, and all these need to be processed by ICT equipment.

Flight booking systems

Passengers can book flights at a travel agent, over the internet or at the airport. ICT systems use a database of aircraft and seat availability that can be accessed from all over the world. By keeping a constant record of booking information from all the places people book tickets, the system ensures that flights cannot be overbooked.

This ICT system also includes other tools, such as:

- Mailing information and tickets to passengers.
- Mailing marketing information, to promote special deals to people who are likely to be interested in them.
- Loyalty systems where regular flyers get points that they can save for free flights and gifts.

Forecasting systems

Airports have summer and winter flight schedules, but often these are not finalised until a few weeks beforehand, and even then may be subject to change. So it is important for the airport to have a plan of how it will meet the expected demand for its services from airlines and passengers.

A forecasting system uses data from previous years and up-to-date booking figures to assess how many passengers and how many flights there will be at a given time. With this information the managers can make sure there are enough staff to deal with passengers effectively.

Desk allocation

Forecasting is very useful in planning check-in desk allocation. An airport has a fixed number of check-in desks. At peak times many people need to use the check-in facilities. The forecasting system will organise a schedule for the desks, following a set of rules devised by the airport manager. A typical list of rules may be something like this:

- Scheduled flights have priority over charter flights.
- Transatlantic flights have priority over other scheduled flights.
- Scheduled flights require two desks, two hours prior to departure.

Using ICT systems the desk allocation for the whole season can be plotted rapidly.

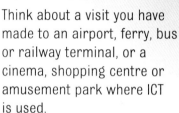
Identifying ICT in use

Think about a visit you have made to an airport, ferry, bus or railway terminal, or a cinema, shopping centre or amusement park where ICT is used.

Make a list of all the different ways you saw ICT being used. Use these headings:

Security
Money
Communication
Transport
Shopping

Staff allocation

Forecasting systems also enable managers to ensure there are enough staff to run the airport efficiently. Handling agents need to make sure that there are sufficient staff available to load and unload baggage from each aircraft. The forecasting system uses data on the number of people required to unload each type of aircraft, and the number of flights, to decide on the number of staff required at different times.

Managers also use the check-in desk allocations to plan how many check-in staff they will need at different times in the season.

Baggage and cargo

Baggage is the luggage passengers take with them on a flight. Cargo is other items carried by the aircraft, for example mail and export goods. ICT is used to ensure that all baggage and cargo gets to the right place.

4 5 6 To ensure that passengers and their baggage travel on the same flight a **bar code** is attached to baggage at check-in. This contains information about the flight taken, the destination and the passenger. A written label is also attached, using letters and colours to identify the airline and the correct flight. The bar code and labels make it easy to identify luggage that is accidentally lost, or that has to be removed from the aeroplane hold because the passenger has not boarded the flight.

Bar codes are also used to label aircraft cargo. The bar code information includes the sender's identity, the recipient's identity, and the date and time for delivery.

The bar codes are read by cordless scanners and laser pens that are not physically linked to a computer system. This means that baggage handlers can check luggage outside the terminal building, rather than having to take all the luggage to a testing point. This saves time and effort in the baggage checking process, and helps staff get luggage to its owners quickly and efficiently.

2 Commercial systems

Airline companies pay to use an airport. The rates the airport charges for different facilities are calculated by ICT commercial systems. Some examples of these charges are:

Runway charges	Each aircraft using a runway is charged according to its weight.
Passenger load supplement	Each aircraft is charged for the number of passengers on board, to cover the cost of terminal facilities.
Apron service charges	Charges for use of airport facilities such as steps or tunnel to an aircraft.
Aircraft parking hours	Aircraft park free for the first two hours. After that they are charged according to aircraft weight.

The computer programs used by commercial systems can calculate these charges for each airline quickly and accurately.

3 Airport information systems

The ICT systems used in an airport need accurate data to perform accurate calculations. The main sources of this data are:

- airline companies
- flight Information Display System
- flight strip recorder
- handling agents.

Flight Information Display System

The Flight Information Display System (FIDS) is 'fed' regularly with data on flight movements. This data includes the flight number, destination and scheduled flight times. Since this data changes frequently, staff have to input the most up-to-date information throughout the day. This information is displayed on overhead monitors in the passenger areas and lounges.

Overhead monitors display up-to-date information on flights.

ICT research

Use Unit 6, the library or the internet to find out more about bar codes and how they work.

Use this information to complete one of the following tasks:

1 Plan and make a display to explain how bar codes work.

2 Create a fact file – a sheet of information with drawings – to explain bar coding.

Flight strip recorder

The Civil Aviation Authority (CAA) operates the flight strip recorder system. This stores information such as the flight number, the actual time of arrival or departure, the runway used, and the flight rules in operation at the time. The records held in the flight strip recorder are also matched with information held in other airport systems to make sure they are up-to-date and accurate. Some of this information is needed to calculate the charges for the airline.

Flights are often delayed, even if only by a few minutes, so the data for the actual times that planes arrive and depart will never exactly match the timetable data. Most computer matching needs data to match with 100% accuracy. Flight strip recorder matching is done using a 'woolly algorithm', which is a set of instructions that attempts to match the data even if it is not exactly the same. This means that the flight data and timetable data can still be matched by the computer, without a human controller getting involved.

Handling agents

The handling agents are responsible for ensuring that passengers and their luggage are moved quickly and efficiently on and off planes. Their ICT systems provide information about the exact number of passengers arriving on a flight and the number of staff required to deal with them and their baggage. Much of this information comes through links with other airport computer systems.

4 Flight planning and control

Air traffic control is one of the most crucial aspects of an airport's operation. The volume of air traffic increases each year and air traffic controllers rely on ICT to keep track of all the aircraft in the airspace above an airport as well as on the ground. Computers alert the controller if a risky or inappropriate command is given. They also monitor aircraft, giving warnings immediately if the aircraft's activity is outside their guidelines. For example, if an aircraft's angle of descent is not correct, or the distance between two aircraft over the airport is not great enough, a warning will sound.

Air traffic controllers also monitor flow control using ICT systems. Flow control matches the number of aircraft in the sky with the number of available landing spots at airports all over the world. Before an aircraft takes off it must tell the destination airport its arrival time. If the destination airport has no runways free for landing at that time, the aircraft cannot take off.

ICT at the airport

1 Describe how an airport uses ICT in:
   - staff allocation
   - flight booking information
   - working out airline charges
   - air traffic control.

2 How do bar codes help handling agents identify a passenger's luggage and the aeroplane it has to be loaded on?

   Why is this information useful?

Air safety

Using the internet or IT-based encyclopaedias, find how air traffic control has developed since the first airports were built. Search for information on the first types of landing aids used by pilots right up to the systems used now.

Produce a short project called **Safety in the skies**.

Include a timeline showing developments in airport-based air traffic control systems.

Import relevant pictures and tables to illustrate your timeline.

Some starting points:
- What is 'the language of the air'?
- How can pilots land in 'zero visibility'?
- Give an example of a 'military' development that has been used in civilian air traffic control.
- Give statistics for one airport's flight movements during a busy period. All major airports have a website that includes this sort of information.

Case study – instant coffee production

The factory featured in this unit employs around 1000 people and produces 530 different products in one main factory complex. The company is one of the world's largest producers of instant coffee. Each year it produces 125 million jars, which is equivalent to more than 10 000 000 000 cups of coffee!

This factory uses ICT systems for communication, data storage, data processing and to control systems. The diagram below shows the flow of information through the business. We will look at how ICT is used in all these areas.

In this unit you will:

- look at how a large factory operates
- find out how ICT is used to make things happen in a food factory.

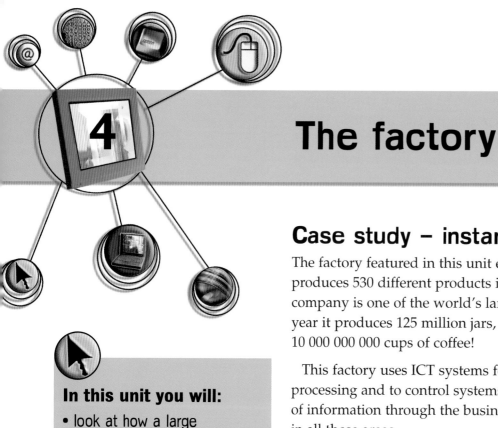

Follow the movement of information from the customer to the factory.

Head office and supermarket link

16 The company head office operates a central **database** that records information about customer orders. Some orders come automatically from customers via a dedicated link. This is a modem or other link using the telephone system, which is reserved only for communication between head office and an important customer.

Large supermarkets have databases of the stock they hold. Their computer systems automatically send out an order when their stock of a product is running low. The system works like this:

5
6
- Each product in the supermarket has a **bar code**. The bar code contains information about where and when the product was manufactured.

6
- At the checkout the **EPOS** (Electronic Point of Sale) system reads the bar code and updates the stock database. For example, every time a jar of coffee is sold the coffee stock in the database is reduced by 1.

- When the stock gets below a certain level the automatic purchasing system sends an order to the manufacturer for a delivery of stock.

This system means the supermarket should never run out of stock. If there is an unexpected change in demand, for example more ice cream being sold in hot weather, the system automatically orders more of the stock needed.

The firewall

The manufacturer needs to ensure that the ordering database is the only part of its ICT system that the supermarket can access. To protect its other systems the head office has a 'firewall' between it and the supermarket. A firewall is a protective system that surrounds the company's ICT systems and prevents unauthorised access. A team of specialist staff work full time to maintain it.

Investigation

Use the library, CD-roms and the internet to find out more about one of the following:

1 Bar codes

What information do product bar codes contain?

What do the numbers and lines on a bar code mean?

2 Firewalls

What is the purpose of a firewall?

Why is a firewall important to companies?

3 EPOS

What is EPOS?

What is the difference between EPOS and EFTPOS?

Production planning

When a supermarket's order arrives at the factory's sales database, the factory's stock database automatically orders the stock needed to complete the order. There may be orders from several different companies. For coffee the glass jar, cap and label have to be ordered. The company making the caps has to order plastic, card and foil; the company making the labels has to order paper, and so on.

It is very important that stock ordered arrives on time, otherwise it may hold up production. Another database, the production database, ensures that the right colour cap, the right jar and the right label come together at the same time.

The sales, stock and production databases communicate with the company's suppliers and ensure that the whole production process runs smoothly.

The factory

In the factory the production equipment is controlled by ICT.

Production control

The coffee production system is controlled from the main control room. This is the most important part of the manufacturing process in this factory. Only people with the correct security pass can use this equipment.

The information about how the coffee is produced is input into the production control system. This information includes:

- the quantity of ingredients
- the grade of coffee required
- parameters for processing, for example heat, time, pressure.

ICT controls the equipment but the product is also checked by hand.

Advantages of using ICT control systems	Disadvantages of using ICT control systems
A computerised control system can monitor many things at a time.	The system is expensive and takes a long time to install.
ICT systems can work 24 hours a day.	The people operating the system will need ongoing training.
High tech systems can work in situations that would be unsafe for people.	Computer-controlled production needs careful advance planning.
The system can be flexible so that the production method can be changed easily.	The system needs to be set up to be flexible so that production methods can be changed easily.

The production control room.

The control system monitors the parameters in the manufacturing process and the safety of the process and displays this information on screen at all times. Fail-safe devices built into the system automatically alter or shut down operations if there is a problem in the process. This way the factory can ensure the product is produced safely and to high quality standards.

The computer screens show charts for each stage of the production process. For example, a pump control shows a diagram of the pump and the vessel the liquid is pumped into. Indicators show the pressure and temperature they should operate at and warn operators if these levels are too high or too low.

The control room staff check the display. If any part of the production goes wrong they use the computer to correct the process. To make this possible the ICT system uses Programmable Logic Control systems (known as PLCs). When a change is made to the process in the control room on a computer the PLC system operates the physical parts of the production system, for example opening and closing valves.

18 Production control in this factory is similar to **control systems** you work with in ICT at school (see Unit 18). You may recognise some of the features: on screen information given as flow diagrams and self-monitoring systems as part of the software and hardware.

Planning the process

Study the list of activities below and write a flowchart showing the order in which they need to be done. Careful! One of these activities must go on all through the other stages. Which is it?

- Check the amount of stock.
- Read customer's order.
- Work out what items are required for the customer's order.
- Receive customer's order.
- Check the quality of the product.
- Order stock from many different supplier companies.
- Select and load the final product for transport.
- Give supplier companies a date by which supplies must be delivered.
- Use the products in the manufacturing process.
- Receive stock.
- Charge the customer.
- Store the finished stock.
- Transport the finished product to the customer.

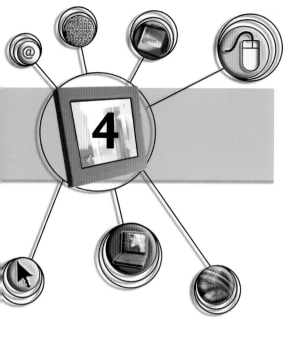

Power supplies

A large factory uses a lot of energy to power its machinery. ICT software is used to ensure that this energy comes from the most cost-effective sources, and plans production so that energy demand can be predicted.

Packing

Even in ICT controlled factories, some parts of the packing are done by hand.

3 5 6   All the products need to be labelled and packed carefully. Each box of jars of coffee has a **bar code** on it. The packers scan the bar code with a laser scanner to find out which pallet each box should be stacked on. Each customer's order is stacked on a separate pallet.

5   **Automatic guided vehicles** (AGVs) take the pallets to the correct dispatch point. From here the products are transported to the supermarket.

Supertags

Supertags are the latest development in bar code technology. Each tag contains a tiny computer chip (in the black spot) and a printed radio antenna (the brown bands). The information in the chip is read by a radio scanner.

Information flow

Produce a flowchart to represent the information flow between supermarkets and manufacturers.

Include notes on your chart to explain:

• How ICT plays a part in the operation of a large factory.

• The benefits of a computer-controlled manufacturing system for the supermarket, the manufacturer and the customer.

• The disadvantages of computer-controlled manufacturing systems.

Compare your flowchart with a friend's.

Discuss any differences in your flowcharts. Why should things happen in the order you have placed them?

An aerial view of the factory complex.

Introducing a computer controlled system

Imagine you are the production director for a food manufacturing company that does not have computer controlled processing.

Produce a presentation describing the reasons for going into computer controlled manufacturing.

Use these headings:

• cost

• disruption

• quality

• flexibility of production

• training

• profit.

Distribution

5

Distribution is concerned with how businesses arrange to get their products delivered to their customers. ICT helps businesses control stock and get their products to the right place on time.

Case study – Ford parts distribution centre, Daventry

Daventry is an ideal location for a distribution centre as it is in the centre of England and close to the M1 motorway and rail links. The Ford parts distribution centre stocks all the spare parts needed for Ford cars, from windscreen wiper blades and oil filters that need to be changed regularly, to larger parts such as body panels, engine blocks or truck axles, that might need to be replaced after an accident.

In this unit you will:

- learn about computerised daily stock order systems
- learn how ICT controls automated guided vehicles.

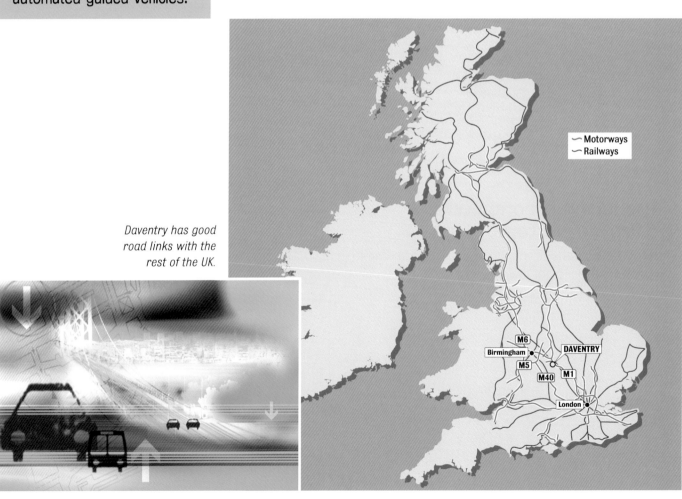

Daventry has good road links with the rest of the UK.

Motorways
Railways

M6
Birmingham
M5
M40 M1
DAVENTRY
London

Computerised daily stock order system

There are around 85 000 Ford parts, so no garage can stock them all. But when a car needs spares, neither the garage nor the car owner wants to have to wait a long time for the parts to arrive.

All Ford dealerships are linked to the distribution centre using a PC and modem. Parts can be ordered electronically until 4 p.m. each day and they usually arrive at the garage within 48 hours. This is called the computerised daily stock order system. With this system the maximum time to supply parts is only four days. Because the supply is so rapid, dealerships have been able to reduce the amount of stock they store by 50 per cent.

When the dealer places the order he or she receives the shipment data online. Shipment data is the details about the order placed, the time it is expected to leave the factory and the time it should be delivered to the dealer.

From this the dealer and customer can know immediately if a part is available and when it will arrive where it is needed.

In the Daventry warehouse all the items are **bar-coded**. As each order is taken from the shelves its bar code is read with a scanner and the central computer stock records are updated. This allows managers to monitor stock levels constantly and automatically reorder parts when stock falls below a certain level.

Automated guided vehicles (AGVs)

ICT controls the **automated guided vehicle** system. When parts arrive at the warehouse they are delivered to the correct space on one of 35 trailers pulled by one of seven 'tugs'. Each tug is guided by electronic impulses transmitted through a wire buried in the floor. The whole system is controlled and monitored by a computer.

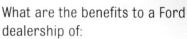

Benefits of ICT

What are the benefits to a Ford dealership of:

a A reduction in the amount of stock stored at the dealership?

b Shipment data giving information on when a part is likely to arrive?

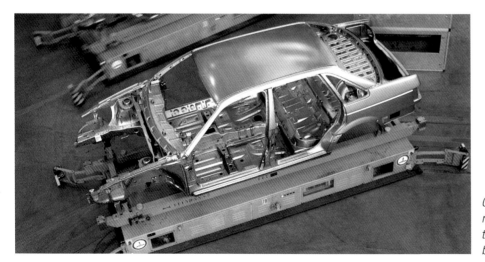

Car parts are moved around the warehouse by AGVs.

FACT FILE

Ford opened the Daventry Distribution Centre in 1968. Since then it has invested a further £12 million to make Daventry the first Ford parts centre to introduce a 'lean' distribution system. This means that stock does not have to be stored for long. All the stock that arrives at the distribution centre has already been allocated to a dealer by the computer, and is quickly sent out to the correct place.

- The Daventry Distribution Centre has 152 500 square metres of covered storage space and holds 85 000 different items.

- More than 60 articulated lorries leave Daventry on the M1 each day.

- Around 44.5 million kilograms of stock are shipped from this centre each year.

- The total value of parts in the Daventry Distribution Centre at any one time is around £132 000 000.

00 Car

Design a car suitable for Jane Pond, a super spy.

Use your imagination to design and label the electronic tools (which may be available now or in the future) that will help her on her missions.

...automatic windscreen wipers, reflating tyres, sensors to match speed of car to speed limit, voice activated systems...

ICT in cars

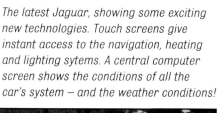

The latest Jaguar, showing some exciting new technologies. Touch screens give instant access to the navigation, heating and lighting sytems. A central computer screen shows the conditions of all the car's system – and the weather conditions!

Robots on the production line.

Investigate the ICT tools used to design or run a modern car and how these have helped cars become:

*   safer
*   easier to drive
*   more comfortable to drive.

Storyboard your ideas for use in a presentation package to show this information to a group of car enthusiasts. Explain in your presentation how you expect ICT tools will improve cars in the next 50 years.

Ordering Ford parts

Using the information in this unit, predict what hardware the dealers and Ford use in the order process.

Draw and label a diagram showing how these pieces of hardware link together. Describe the function of each piece of hardware in the overall process.

Start from when a customer arrives in a Ford dealership wanting a part. Finish where the part is delivered.

The supermarket

In this unit you will:

- learn about bar codes and scanning, EPOS and EFTPOS
- find out about sales-based ordering and stock control
- discover how ICT benefits the retailer and the customer.

All aspects of business in a large supermarket are either controlled or monitored by ICT, for example:

- stock levels/stock control
- stock distribution
- payroll
- accounts
- store planning
- branch and product performance.

In this chapter you will discover how the supermarket chain Tesco uses ICT to help serve customers efficiently.

At the checkout

What we used to call a till is now called an Electronic Point of Sale system or EPOS. The checkout assistant passes each item of shopping over a laser scanner. The scanner identifies the product from the bar code and transmits this information to the store's central computer. The store's central computer database has a description and the price of every item on sale. This information is transmitted back to the checkout and is printed on the customer's receipt.

EPOS

The EPOS system has many advantages for the customer and for the store. These are explained over the next few pages.

EPOS can run special promotions called multisavers. For a 'buy two get one free' offer the EPOS machine recognises when a customer has bought three of an item and does not charge for the third one.

Self-scanning

Some supermarkets have a self-scanning system. Customers use a hand-held scanner unit to scan the bar codes of the items they put in their trolley. At the checkout they hand the scanner to the operator who then displays the total price. The customer then pays in the normal way. Since the purchases are only handled once it is much quicker.

Customer benefits

1 Discuss this list with a friend. Which of these are guaranteed by EPOS?

- Accuracy – fewer mistakes
- Easier packing
- Improved customer service
- Faster service
- Shorter queues at the checkout
- Itemised till receipts

2 Why do you think some supermarkets have introduced self-scanning?

What are the advantages and disadvantages of self-scanning for a store?

Bar codes

The first two numbers represent the country of origin, the next five represent the suppliers and the last five represent the product. The last digit is a 'check' digit.

A **bar code** is a unique combination of thick and thin lines found on almost every product today. The idea originally came from Switzerland but it was developed in the US.

Every product has a European Article Number (EAN) which is represented by the bar code and also written below it. It is usually 13 digits but can be 8 on some products.

Stock control

The average supermarket now stocks about 40 000 items or lines, compared with just 5000 in 1983. Keeping track of all this stock would be impossible without ICT. EPOS constantly feeds back information to the store's main computer, so managers can know at any time how much has been sold and how much of a line they have in stock. When stocks get low the **sales-based ordering system** orders more from the supplier. This system helps to ensure the supermarket does not run out of stock, and also means that the stores do not order stock until they need it, so fresh foods do not have to be stored for long.

Pricing

All prices are input into the store's main computer, so individual items do not need price labels. If the price changes the staff just change the label on the shelving. Fresh goods sold by weight, such as cheese, are still individually priced by staff, as they need to be cut and weighed in a very clean environment. Fruit and vegetables are weighed at the checkout and the computer calculates the price due.

Customer payment

Many customers now pay using Electronic Funds Transfer at Point of Sale or EFTPOS. This allows money to be transferred direct from the customer's bank account into Tesco's bank account. Each EFTPOS machine in the store is in direct contact with the customer's bank. Each transaction is checked at the bank. If the customer does not have enough money in the bank, the bank does not allow the purchase.

EFTPOS also allows the customer to get 'cashback' – to draw out cash direct from their bank or credit card account. The transaction is checked at the bank before it goes ahead.

Prices are shown on the shelves.

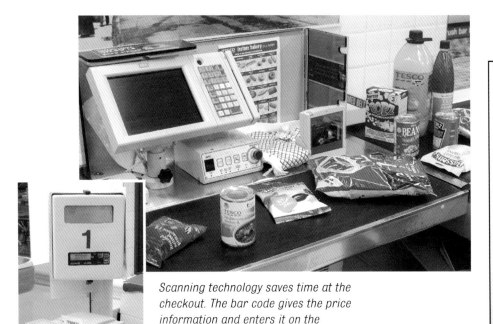

Scanning technology saves time at the checkout. The bar code gives the price information and enters it on the customer's bill.

Inputs and outputs in a supermarket

1 List all the input and output devices shown in the photograph of the supermarket checkout.

Input device	Output device

2 What output device do you think drives the moving belt?

3 How important is the human operator in this system?

4 How could the system work without the operator?

Loyalty cards

When Tesco stores started they were the first supermarkets to give 'Green Shield Stamps'. Customers collected stamps depending on the amount of money they spent and stuck them into books. These could then be exchanged for goods at special catalogue shops.

The loyalty card is the modern equivalent. At each purchase the card is swiped and the number of points gained is stored on the computer.

Every few months the customer receives vouchers and money-off coupons for Tesco stores. As well as benefiting the customer, this scheme allows the store to identify and analyse each customer's purchases, so they can target new products and advertising at customers they think may be interested.

Tesco also runs Clubcard plus accounts. Customers pay money into the Clubcard account each month. When they pay for their shopping with this card they also get double Clubcard points. Each month Tesco pays the customer a small amount of interest on the money in the Clubcard plus account.

Customer service

With a large number of customers, Tesco needs to use ICT in its customer service department.

Most people contact the customer service centre by telephone. An interactive voice response (IVR) filters out calls that can be handled without an operator. An automatic call distribution (ACD) system routes other calls to available operators to reduce caller waiting times. Calls do not arrive in the same quantity throughout the day or week so a call forecasting and scheduling system (QMax) forecasts when most calls are likely and decides how many operators will be needed.

Each operator has access to an intranet which contains the answers to frequently asked questions. The operators also log each enquiry so that management can be kept up-to-date on customer concerns.

Operators deal with thousands of enquiries each day.

Payment methods

1 Fill in the table of advantages of these services to the customer and to the store.

	Advantage to customer	Advantage to store
EFTPOS		
Cashback		

2 Why do supermarkets use customer loyalty cards?

3 Look back at Unit 4. Draw a diagram showing the links between supermarkets, banks and factories.

Customer information

1 Imagine that you are a supermarket manager. You are about to introduce self-scanning in your store. Design a poster for display in the store to inform your customers about the new service.

2 You work in a supermarket customer service department. You have received a letter from an elderly man who uses your store but is worried about the new self-scanning. He does not understand the system and thinks it is a waste of money.

Write him a letter to reassure him about the system and explain its benefits.

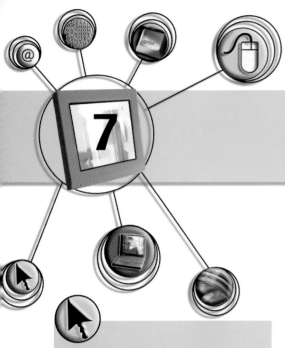

The Internet

The Internet is the most powerful tool for worldwide communication that has ever existed. It gives individuals opportunities to access large amounts of information, to meet new people, to play games, to read and to shop online. Businesses can use the Internet to advertise their products cheaply all over the world, in what has become known as the global marketplace.

In this unit you will:

- gain an understanding of how the Internet works
- explore what the Internet is useful for
- discover how the Internet can spread computer viruses.

What is the Internet?

Most computer users would picture the millions of web pages available online, but this is not the Internet. The Internet is the largest wide area network (WAN) in the world. A wide area network is a network of computers connected over large distances via telephone systems. Individuals and companies can connect to this network to access and share information with others worldwide.

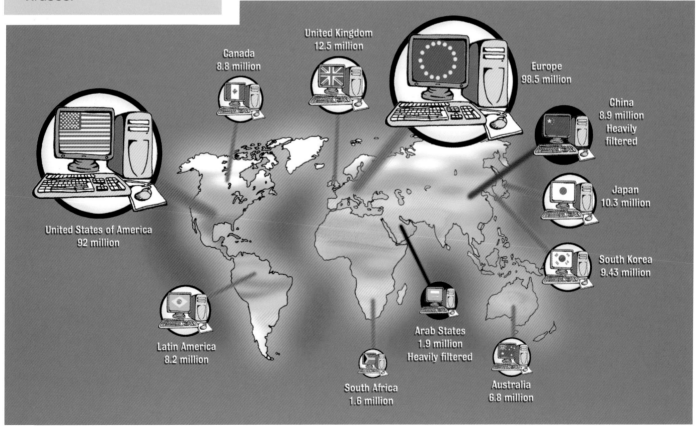

Internet connections around the world (2002).

The Internet concept was first tested by the United States Department of Defense in the 1960s as a communication tool, but on a much smaller scale. The global network of computers we now call the Internet has been developed since the early 1990s.

The World Wide Web

The World Wide Web (WWW) is the collection of websites that Internet users can view. Each website is made up of web pages. Computers holding web pages and connected to the Internet are called web servers. To view these pages on a PC you use software called a web browser, that can request pages from a web server. The browser then interprets the instructions contained within a web page and displays the information on screen. The two most common web browsers are *Internet Explorer* and *Netscape*.

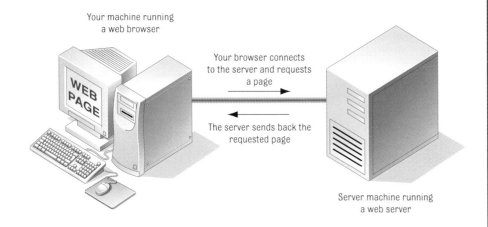

Your machine running a web browser

WEB PAGE

Your browser connects to the server and requests a page

The server sends back the requested page

Server machine running a web server

Using the WWW

1 Use the information in Units 20, 21 and 22 to help you list all the different types of things you can do on the WWW.

Write a brief explanation of each entry in your list.

2 How could these people use the facilities you have described in question 1?

- Teachers
- People in business
- School students
- University students
- Parents

3 Why do you think the WWW has grown so rapidly?

The WWW is like the biggest library in the world, with thousands of websites, some with hundreds of pages of information, available for everyone to use. It has developed extremely fast and could grow much more, because it allows individuals and companies to share information cheaply. This is why so many people and businesses now use the Internet and more and more have their own websites. These add to the collection of personal, financial and factual information that makes the Web such a rich place for investigation.

How web technology works

The process that allows web users to access information on the WWW is very simple. It all starts in a home or office with the click of a mouse button.

The most common way to connect to the Internet is by using an Internet Service Provider (ISP). An ISP is a company that provides a gateway to the global network of computers. There are a lot of different ISPs, for example AOL, Freeserve, NTL.

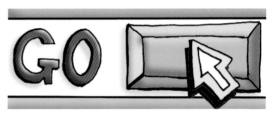

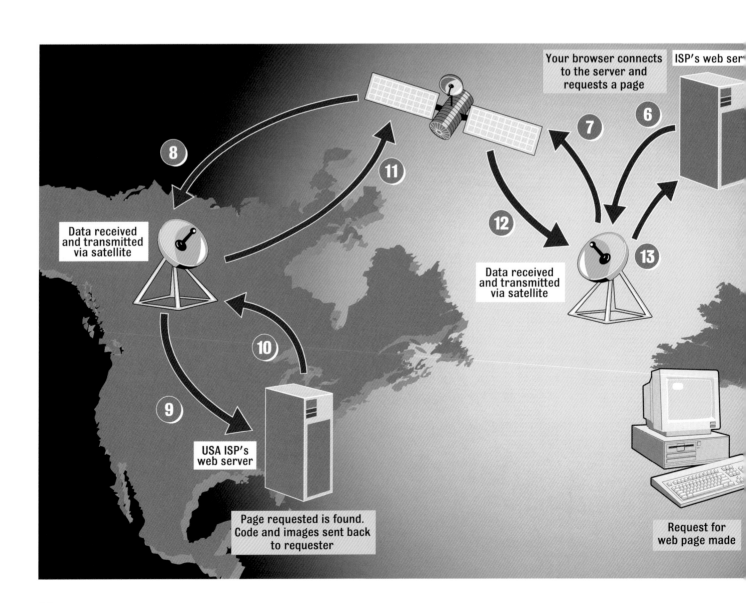

Your browser connects to the server and requests a page

ISP's web ser

Data received and transmitted via satellite

Data received and transmitted via satellite

USA ISP's web server

Page requested is found. Code and images sent back to requester

Request for web page made

Problems with the Internet

As with all technologies, things don't always go smoothly. Sometimes a web page may take a long time to display on your computer screen, particularly if it contains complex images. Also, if you are researching a particular topic it can be difficult to find websites that are relevant.

Learning to deal with these problems is all part of the Internet experience. You can learn skills to help you use the WWW effectively in Units 20 and 21.

Who owns the Internet?

No one person or organisation owns the Internet. It is made up of many ISP companies, who each have millions of customers who contribute pages to the WWW. It is easy for Internet users to place web pages on the WWW, but it is difficult for ISPs to control the content and quality of these sites.

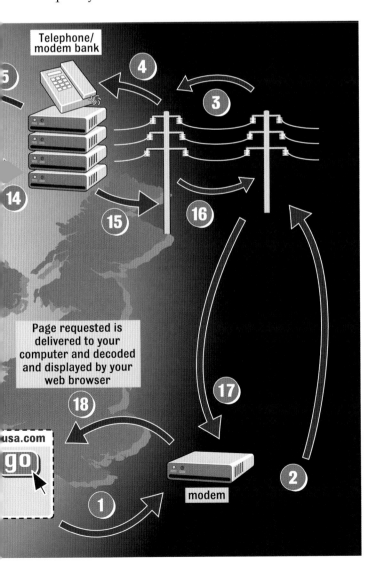

Suppose you want to view a web page held on a computer in the United States. What happens next?

1   User requests access to a web page using a web browser by typing in the web page address.

2–5   The request travels via the telephone system to an ISP. The ISP connects you to the Internet.

6–9   From the ISP the request travels to the US and the computer where the page is stored.

10–18   If the request is accepted the information travels back through the system to your computer. All this takes just a few seconds.

Negative uses of the Internet

Because it is easy to access the Internet, some people use the WWW to pass on information that is poorly researched or against the law. Others create viruses, hack into computer systems, or send email 'bombs' that may interfere with computer systems. Fortunately only a small number of users abuse the freedom to communicate that the Internet provides.

Computer viruses

Computer viruses are small computer programs that can harm files on other computer systems. A virus is unlikely to damage the computer hardware. However losing computer data is very serious, especially for businesses, and could cost a company millions of pounds.

The Internet does not create viruses but it can be used to transmit them across the globe, making them a serious threat to other Internet users.

People create computer viruses for many reasons. Some are written by employees of firms who are upset in some way, as a way of getting back at the company. Others just want to see if they can use their programming talents to an unproductive and harmful end. Creating a computer virus is not illegal, but distributing it on the Internet is, and can lead to a criminal prosecution. Most countries now have specialist police forces who track criminals who misuse the Internet.

Hacking

Hackers access files that are supposedly locked away from public viewing. They see it as a challenge to gain access to this information. Hackers are computer users with a considerable amount of skill. They claim that hacking is useful because learning how to hack also teaches you how to protect your systems from other hackers.

Some hackers believe that all information should be available to everyone who wishes to see it, and resent the fact that the Internet is run as a business by businesses (ISPs). They also feel that it is unfair that big businesses can make more use of the Internet because they can buy expensive technology that uses the Internet more effectively. For these reasons hackers often target large businesses.

Hackers are seen as a negative product of the Internet because their activities can cause loss of data, and in business data is money.

Internet ideas

Write a short passage expressing your view on the following issues.

1 Are hackers and virus creators cool and clever, or destructive and undesirable?

2 The WWW is a way of expressing opinions, free from government influence and politics.

3 The WWW and Internet make crime and criminal activity easier.

4 The Internet and WWW are the most effective ways of sharing information for the benefit of all the peoples of the world.

5 The Internet and WWW have helped to make life easier and will continue to do so.

Other uses of the Internet

The WWW is full of websites which may be informative or fun:

- chat rooms
- news groups
- mailing lists
- online libraries
- games play
- online communities
- online education.

Find out more about these in Unit 20. Always remember to be safe when using the Internet. Follow the netiquette rules (see page 154).

e-commerce

e-commerce is short for electronic commerce. This means the buying and selling of products and services by businesses and consumers over the Internet. Many types of business are involved in e-commerce, from individual one-person businesses to large international corporations. Whatever the size of the organisation, they all recognise one thing: that the Internet means big business.

Shopping from home.

Businesses sell over the Internet because:

- The Internet and WWW make a product or service available to millions of people worldwide. This large market means that sales should increase.

- It costs much less to set up a website than to set up a shop to sell from.

- e-commerce communication is fast and efficient. The information about products and offers can be updated frequently.

Customers buy goods and services over the Internet because:

- It is convenient. Customers can order online and receive the goods the next day without leaving the comfort of their home or office.

- Customers can compare prices on other company's websites before they purchase. So they can make sure they get the best deal available at the time.

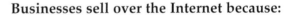

Buying goods over the Internet

Most websites offering online purchasing have a **secure site**. Secure site systems are very expensive, but they protect customer information from hackers. This could be personal information about your lifestyle, your passwords or even your credit card details.

Most customers use credit cards to buy goods over the Internet. However some companies, especially in share trading, hold an account for you. You deposit money in the account and you can then spend it on their website.

FACT FILE

- In 1997, 36 million people worldwide were connected to the Internet.

  In 2001, 513.41 million people used the Internet on a regular basis.

  This number is expected to continue to double every year.

- In 1999, 25% of Internet users had already used e-commerce to purchase goods or services.

  In 2001, surveys showed that 47% of Internet users had made at least one purchase online.

The Internet in business

1 Your boss has asked you to comment on a report she is writing.
  In it she has stated that:

  a The WWW and the Internet are the same thing.

  b The Internet is so small that it is currently not worth having a company website to sell products from.

  c Staff should not contact the company's US office via the Internet, because most Internet users are hackers who would put viruses into the company's computer system.

  d The Internet has no real benefits for the company.

  Write a response to your boss, explaining why these phrases are incorrect.

2 What is meant by the global marketplace? How could a business use the Internet to reach more customers?

Internet presentation

1 Make a presentation about the Internet. Design slides to show:

  a A visual representation of the global network of computers.

  b Easy to understand definitions of
  - ISPs
  - web browsers
  - hackers
  - viruses
  - websites and web pages.

  c The benefits and drawbacks of using the Internet.

2 Keep a record of Internet pages you view. Give each page marks out of 10 for:

  How easy it was to find the page
  Interest
  How easy the page is to read
  How quickly the page loads
  The quality of the information

The lighthouse

8

In this unit you will:

• learn about a system of warning beacons controlled from one mainland station.

From the sixteenth century until quite recently, lighthouse keepers lived a lonely life in isolated parts of the coastline and on rocks and islands out at sea, keeping a light burning to warn ships of danger. But now lighthouses are controlled automatically from a station on the mainland, and there is no need for live-in keepers. The last lighthouse in the UK to become automatic was North Foreland Lighthouse in Kent. Its keepers left on 26 November 1998.

Bishop Rock Lighthouse, 4 miles west of the Scilly Isles.

The lighthouse service

Lighthouses guide and warn ships of danger in coastal waters 24 hours a day, 365 days a year, in all weathers. Their shape and colours make them stand out from their surroundings so that they can be seen easily. Each lighthouse flashes in a pattern of a different number of flashes per minute, known as its 'characteristic'. This enables sailors to identify which lighthouse they are passing.

In poor visibility lighthouses transmit warning radio signals and their fog signals give sound warnings. They provide an essential service, so it is vital that they function reliably.

Automating lighthouses

Trinity House Lighthouse is the lighthouse authority for England, Wales, the Channel Islands and Gibraltar. The company was given a Royal Charter by Henry VIII in 1514. They started converting their lighthouses to automatic operation in the early 1980s, and now all 69 of their UK lighthouses are automatic.

Two major advances in technology have made it possible to automate lighthouses.

1 ICT **monitoring and control programs** that control the lighthouse systems via radio links and the telephone lines from a main base in Essex. From here all the 69 lighthouses are controlled and monitored, and any faults in them are diagnosed.

2 Lantern top helipads – helicopter landing areas built above the lighthouse lantern. This means that maintenance and service teams can fly by helicopter to the lighthouse when repairs are necessary.

Automated systems in a lighthouse

All the Trinity House lighthouses contain the same standard equipment, which is checked at regular intervals 24 hours a day from the Control Centre at Harwich.

If a systems fails the telemetry equipment in the lighthouse is activated and details are automatically sent to Harwich. The information is transmitted using telephone lines, mobile phones or radio, depending upon the location of the lighthouse. The control centre immediately sends the closest service team by helicopter to repair the faulty systems.

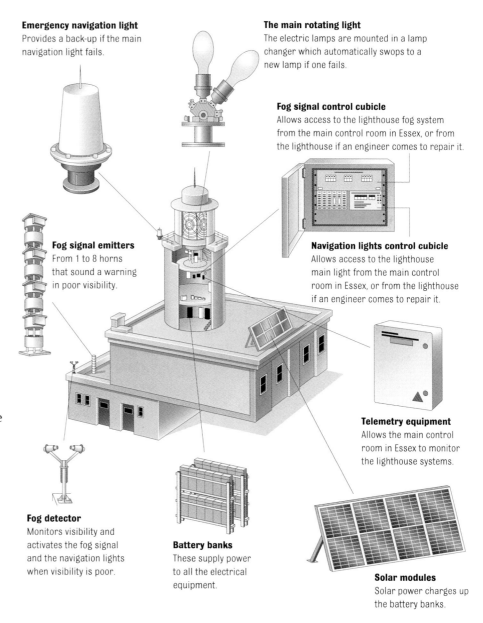

Emergency navigation light
Provides a back-up if the main navigation light fails.

The main rotating light
The electric lamps are mounted in a lamp changer which automatically swops to a new lamp if one fails.

Fog signal control cubicle
Allows access to the lighthouse fog system from the main control room in Essex, or from the lighthouse if an engineer comes to repair it.

Fog signal emitters
From 1 to 8 horns that sound a warning in poor visibility.

Navigation lights control cubicle
Allows access to the lighthouse main light from the main control room in Essex, or from the lighthouse if an engineer comes to repair it.

Telemetry equipment
Allows the main control room in Essex to monitor the lighthouse systems.

Fog detector
Monitors visibility and activates the fog signal and the navigation lights when visibility is poor.

Battery banks
These supply power to all the electrical equipment.

Solar modules
Solar power charges up the battery banks.

St Catherine's lighthouse, Isle of Wight.

Saving money

Automating a lighthouse is extremely expensive, but it actually saves money in the long term. As an example, St. Catherine's lighthouse on the southern tip of the Isle of Wight cost £95 000 to automate. The equipment is expected to last for 15 years, and over this time £800 000 will be saved. Most of these savings come from reducing staff numbers, so the salaries bill is much lower. At St Catherine's it has also been possible to sell the former lighthouse keeper's house.

Global Positioning System

GPS uses satellites for land and sea navigation.

Lighthouses also have a new role for the twenty-first century. As well as warning shipping about dangerous rocks and channels, they can help boats to pinpoint their position on a map, using the Global Positioning System (GPS). This was originally developed by the US Department of Defense for military use.

GPS uses 24 satellites which orbit the earth and transmit radio signals. Ships with GPS equipment can receive signals from at least three of these satellites wherever they are. From these signals the GPS can calculate the position of the ship in degrees longitude and latitude, to within 100 metres.

In very dangerous areas of water a ship may need to know its position even more accurately. For this reason 12 lighthouses around the coast of the UK have become GPS transmitting stations. Using signals from these as well as from the orbiting satellites, the ship's GPS can pinpoint the position much more exactly and so avoid rocks or other dangers.

All boats with receiving equipment can use this service for free. It is financed by small charges on commercial shipping.

GPS receiving equipment. GPS is used in car navigation systems, as well as in boats.

Navigation

1 What are the advantages of automating lighthouses?
2 What is meant by a lighthouse's 'characteristics'?
3 Why are lighthouse characteristics important?
4 What does GPS stand for?
5 In what other situations in everyday life could the GPS systems be used?

Using technology

1 Use the internet to find out more about how these work:
   • Global Positioning Systems
   • Bank Automatic Teller Machines (ATMs)
   • cell phones
   • satellites.
2 Write a short newspaper article discussing some of the ways that ICT benefits society. Use some of the information you found in question 1 as examples.

9

The newspaper

Computer technology has had a very big impact on newspaper production. When it was introduced it changed the ways in which people in this industry had been working for generations.

In this unit you will:
- learn how ICT is used to create a newspaper.

Printing newspapers.

Newspaper production

Before computer technology was developed, journalists wrote the news stories either by hand or using a typewriter. The editor checked what the journalists had written and marked by hand any corrections to be made. To print the story the text had to be pieced together word by word using metal type. This was known as 'typesetting'. It was very time consuming and letters could easily be set in the wrong order, creating mistakes.

The first big technological development was photocomposition, developed in the mid 20th century. In this method text was typed by an operator and later transferred to printing drums using a photographic method. These drums were then used in printing presses to print the words and pictures on to paper.

Nowadays journalists write their articles on a computer and these are transferred directly into a publishing package where all the pages are laid out. Photographs are positioned at this stage and the text edited to fit in the space available. These pages are then sent as computer files to the printers, who now are more likely to use laser printers than mechanical printing presses to print on to paper

People working in the newspaper industry did not welcome the new ICT systems at first. They were worried that many of the workers in the traditional jobs would be made redundant. However the ICT revolution has secured jobs, as it has helped newspapers to compete with television in producing words and pictures on the latest news, often in full colour. Employers have been forced to retrain their workforce in the new technology.

In the next sections you will see how word processing and publishing packages, computer controlled machinery and satellite communications have all changed the way in which newspapers are produced.

Changing newspaper styles.

Changes in the newspaper industry

1 Find news articles about the changes in newspaper printing over the last century.

Create a display to show how the newspaper has developed over time. Display information about:

- How newspapers have always used the new technologies of the time.
- What the first newspapers were like.
- How today's newspapers use computers, digital cameras and other electronic equipment.

Create a timeline that shows the technological developments from the first newspaper to the current day.

Point out where the most development has occurred.

2 Imagine you are a newspaper owner in the 1970s.

Write a report for your staff recommending that the newspaper should start using new technology. List all the advantages of using the technology as key points. Back up your points with details.

The impact of new technology

Prepare arguments for a debate about the impact new technologies have had on society. Think of arguments in favour of new technology and against it. You can use information on ICT systems from other units in Section A to support your views.

Parts of a newspaper

A newspaper contains:

1 News stories and reports. The newspaper has to be able to react very quickly to changing events and report on them swiftly so that the stories it prints are up to date.

2 Articles and features that have been planned in advance. These may be of general interest, e.g. fashion, health and beauty, or based on events in the lead news items, e.g. profiles of election candidates or sports personalities.

3 Advertising. Companies pay a lot of money to advertise in a national newspaper.

News sources

News reporting has benefited enormously from ICT.

The news stories and reports in a newspaper are written by journalists. Some journalists work directly for the newspaper. Others are freelance and sell their stories to a newspaper. As everybody expects to see pictures with the news stories, journalists are usually accompanied by photographers. Some journalists (known as photojournalists) take their own photographs.

Newspapers also buy news stories from news agencies. The agencies have journalists based all over the world. When something newsworthy happens, their nearest reporter can go quickly to the scene and send accurate, up-to-the-minute information back to the agency.

Large news corporations own several different newspapers, often in different countries. The largest of these is News Corporation, which owns *The Sun*, *The Times* and the *News of the World* in the UK, as well as newspapers in the US and Australasia. Corporations of this size may have their own jet aircraft and helicopters to get their journalists on the spot very quickly when a news story breaks.

Once the journalist has the story, he or she needs to get it to the newspaper editor in time for the next morning's paper. Journalists can write their reports on a laptop computer and send them to the editor from any part of the world in seconds, by linking the computer to a mobile phone or via satellite link. In the same way, photographs taken with a digital camera may be sent as image files. So communications technology is essential to the modern journalist. After all, the newspaper that is first with the big story will sell the most newspapers that day.

War comes to America

The Sunday Times • October 14, 2001

FOOTBALL 7

Simply the best ?

He's the man with the golden touch, owner of the most fevered lust of the game. **Rob Hughes** assesses whether David Beckham is the best in the world

Diligent youth gets his Reward

Hard work and love of the game make Beckham the player he is today, says **Jonathan Northwood**

News images

Before digital cameras were invented, printing photographs in newspapers was a lengthy procedure. First the film had to be removed from the camera and developed as negatives. Prints were then made from these, on photographic paper. When the whole newspaper page, including photographs, had been laid out it was etched on to thin aluminium plates, which were then used to transfer the print and images on to paper.

Digital photography means that images can be:

● Input into the newspaper layout as image files. There is no need to print the photographs first.

● Enhanced to improve the quality.

● Cropped and sized as required to fit the page.

● Sent anywhere in the world in seconds.

Image files can be stored so that the picture can be used again and again. In a newspaper if you see the caption 'library picture' underneath a picture this means that the picture was not taken at the same time or place as the article it appears with. Some photographs are often needed, such as photographs of politicians, soap stars and members of the royal family. Using photographs from the newspaper's own library saves the newspaper money.

Photo libraries store a wide range of photographs. All the images are referenced with key words on a database, so you can search easily for photos on any topic. The photo library charges a fee each time a photo is used.

Digital images

1 What are the main advantages of using digital images for the news? How are digital images better than conventional photographs? Consider these points:

   • How the pictures can be sent where they are needed.

   • How easy it is to copy, crop or manipulate the image to suit the editor's needs.

2 Ask your teacher to show you how to use a digital camera.

   Write three short pieces as part of a training course for new journalists explaining:

   a How to use a digital camera

   b How to download the digital image

   c How to send the digital image to the office using email.

3 Explain the drawbacks of using digital images in the following situations.

   • Reporter's camera batteries run out

   • Reporter drops camera with digital images still inside

   • The communications systems (telephone, satellite) are out of action in the country where the reporter is based.

Creating the page layout

The production team lays out each page of the newspaper so that articles are with their photographs and arranged so they are easy to read. Each member of the team has a screen large enough to display a full newspaper page. The computer operator and the editor work together on the display to create pages, using the company's Local Area Network (LAN). This is a network of computers connected by wires over a small distance, so that users can share files.

Producing the pages of a newspaper requires skill. Each news report is read to assess how serious and how important the story it is, before deciding where to put it on a page. Sometimes journalists lay out their own text and photographs. This way they can give readers the freshness of their first-hand impressions of the news.

Computer technology enables journalists, editors and production staff to produce high quality newspapers containing the latest news and photographs. The same technology also streamlines the production process. Fewer people are involved in creating each newspaper page and each stage of production is less time consuming using ICT.

Printing the newspaper

When the pages are completed they are sent to the printing plants. If these are far away, satellite communication technology is used to transfer copies of the computer files.

Creating newspaper pages on screen.

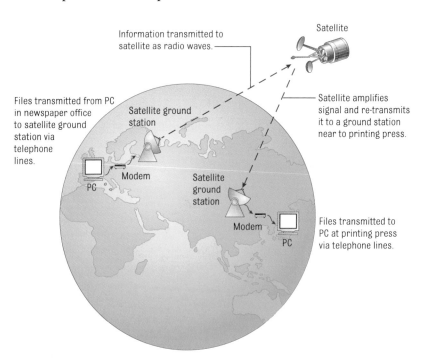

Information transmitted to satellite as radio waves.

Satellite

Satellite amplifies signal and re-transmits it to a ground station near to printing press.

Files transmitted from PC in newspaper office to satellite ground station via telephone lines.

Satellite ground station

Modem

PC

Satellite ground station

Modem

PC

Files transmitted to PC at printing press via telephone lines.

Newspapers need to be printed very quickly, or they will be out of date before they are put on sale. It takes 18 hours to produce a typical newspaper from start to finish, though during that time the news articles and images may be altered many times before the newspaper is printed. Because this process is repeated almost every day of the year, it has to be cheap and reliable. It also needs to be capable of producing high quality readable newspapers with colour photographs.

All stages of the print process are automatic and controlled by a computer. Automatic paper feeders feed in the paper for printing and automatic rotary presses transfer the print to the page, using a rotating cylinder. Computers ensure that the paper comes into contact with the rotating cylinder at the correct time, so that the pages are printed accurately. The presses can print in colour on both sides of the paper simultaneously and can print up to 150 000 copies per hour.

At the end of the printing line the papers are tied in bundles by a machine. The papers for different areas are bundled separately, ready to be sent to their distribution zones.

Communications technology means that newspapers can be printed in two or more places at the same time to make distribution easier. A newspaper that is published in Japan can be printed simultaneously in England, the USA and other countries. The same technology also allows ships at sea to print out daily newspapers for passengers and crew on a long voyage.

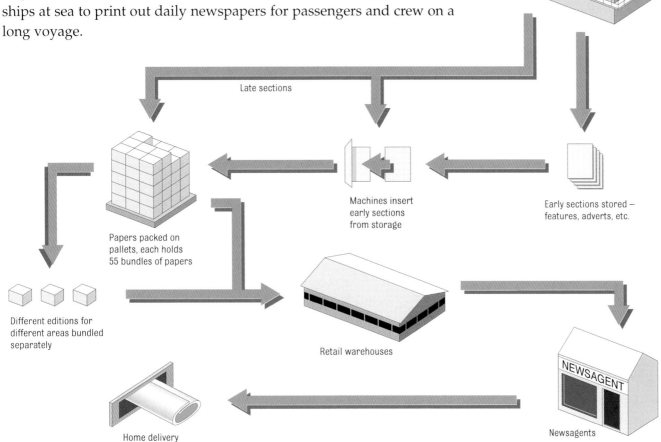

Printers

Late sections

Machines insert early sections from storage

Early sections stored – features, adverts, etc.

Papers packed on pallets, each holds 55 bundles of papers

Different editions for different areas bundled separately

Retail warehouses

Home delivery

NEWSAGENT

Newsagents

Electronic newspapers

As technology develops, the news business is expanding beyond the printed page. All the national newspapers in the UK have a website where you can read a virtual newspaper. The news and features from the day's paper are available to read online. This is not really a 'newspaper', but it has some advantages. Most people do not read all of a newspaper; they have 'favourite' sections. With the virtual newspaper can go straight to the parts you want and read them on screen, saving paper and ink, and a trip to the newsagent! You can also use the **search facilities** on the newspaper website to find articles on a particular subject or from a particular period.

21

Electronic ink

The newspaper industry is continually investigating new technology to help it compete with radio, TV and the Internet. One of the latest innovations is electronic ink technology. Its developers believe that people prefer to read large amounts of text from paper, rather than computer screens.

The electronic ink is used to coat plastic sheets. The sheets are thin and flexible, like paper. The ink consists of tiny transparent spheres, known as microcapsules, each containing microscopic black and white balls.

A grid of these microcapsules can form one letter. The photograph shows just one part of the grid for a single letter e. When an electric current is applied to the ink, the different coloured balls in the microcapsules rise or sink. By altering the electric current applied you can make each microcapsule either white or black, to form different letters. In this way you can reproducce pages of text on the plastic sheets.

In the future you will be able to have your own set of plastic sheets coated with electronic ink and download the latest news on to them electronically each day. The sheets can be used again and again – every time you download new text it will simply replace the text from the previous day. However, the technology for this has not yet been developed.

Mixing electronic ink.

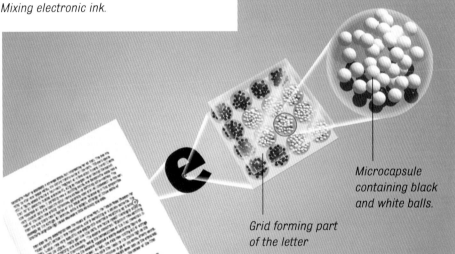

Microcapsule containing black and white balls.

Grid forming part of the letter

ICT and the newspaper industry

1 List the advantages and disadvantages of a virtual newspaper.

2 Ask your teacher to print information from the Internet about the development of electronic ink. How do you think this will affect the newspaper industry?

3 Do you think that the development of electronic ink will spell the end for virtual newspapers?

4 Do you think the development of electronic ink will affect the newspaper industry in a similar way to the technological developments of the past? Consider these points:

• Loss of jobs in the industry

• Ability to deliver the news faster and more frequently.

Making the news

Choose one of the following:

1 Create a newspaper page of your own. Write your own news stories, features and advertisements and use appropriate images.

2 Use a digital camera to take pictures of your school and the local area.

• Create a library index system for your pictures.

• What categories will you list them in? For example, for the school pictures you could have categories buildings, year 8 pupils, science laboratories, etc.

• Why will you need cross-references between categories? Use some of your photographs to create one of these:

- A virtual school tour

- A presentation about your local area

- A leaflet about places of historical interest in your area

- A website for visitors to your area. Include a map with photographs of the points of interest.

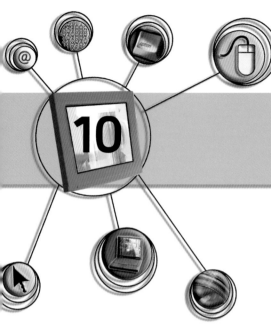

Capturing weather data

10

Data capture is all about collecting data for processing and analysing by a computer. This data may be collected by many different data capture devices.

The Meteorogical Office

The Meteorological Office (Met Office) is one of the largest collectors of data in the UK. It is responsible for keeping long-term records about the weather and climate. These records are stored in the National Archive and are used to:

- Prepare weather forecasts.
- Inform farmers about changing weather and climate patterns that could affect their decisions on which crops to plant.
- Provide information for town planners, for example if a particular site is likely to flood frequently.

The Met Office also collects data on health. These records can help doctors understand when certain types of illness are likely to occur, and help them to plan for these times. An example is influenza, which is most common in the cold, wet winter months.

Clearly, the data the Met Office uses for its predictions has to be accurate. Met Office data is collected in weather stations around the country. For a station to be accepted to provide data for the National Archive it has to have equipment of an approved design, installed according to Met Office guidelines. The station also has to be able to record observations at specific times of the day. These restrictions help to ensure that all the data sent to the National Archive is accurate and reliable.

Weather stations

The Met Office has a network of weather stations around the UK, in towns, cities and the countryside. Most of these are fully automated and take regular observations and measurements, which they transmit to the Met Office for use in weather forecasting.

There are two types of weather station in the network:

1 Stations owned and operated by the Met Office.

In this unit you will:
- learn how the Meteorological Office collects weather and climate data.

2 Voluntary stations, owned by individuals and companies. These also send data to the Met Office. Universities often own weather stations and use the data in their research. Schools may also have their own weather station for data collection and other educational projects. Some individuals interested in meteorology also have weather stations.

Weather observations

A standard weather station measures rainfall using a rain gauge. It also contains a data logger and a thermometer.

The data logger is the most important unit, as it processes and stores the data from the measuring devices in the weather station. Loggers can usually store several weeks' worth of data. Regular backups have to be made to ensure the data is not lost.

The data logger has an internal clock, so that all measurements are taken at exactly the same time at all the UK weather stations. The data collected is sent automatically to the Met Office by PCs connected to the weather stations.

Stations must be checked regularly to ensure the equipment is operating effectively.

FACT FILE

- 5000 voluntary stations record data about rainfall. This data is sent to the Met Office every month.
- 500 weather stations make observations of temperature, humidity, wind speed and direction, cloud amount, visibility and sunshine as well as rainfall. This information is sent to the Met Office each day.
- Some stations record additional details about soil temperature and solar radiation. This is useful for the horticulture, forestry and agriculture industries.

Measuring temperature

Air temperature and soil temperature are measured using electrical thermometers which provide readings from sensors. These are calibrated (checked for accuracy) on a regular basis.

These sensors have to be installed carefully to ensure that they are not affected by other heat sources, such as electrical cabling or sunlight. A Stevenson thermometer screen is used inside the weather station to keep direct sunlight off the thermometers. This is simply a wooden box, painted white to reflect the sun's rays. Any electrical cabling must be installed carefully to ensure it cannot affect the thermometer. If such precautions are not taken, the temperature readings will be inaccurate.

All the temperature readings are fed into the data logger.

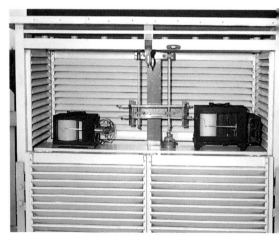

Stevenson thermometer screen.

Measuring rainfall

Rainfall is usually measured with a tipping bucket rain gauge. This has two buckets which fill in turn as it rains. When one bucket is full, the weight of the rainwater tips it up, emptying it. Meanwhile the other bucket starts to fill up. This cycle is repeated while it continues to rain. Each time a bucket tips it triggers a sensor which reports 0.2 mm of rainfall to the data logger. From this information the data logger can provide the Met Office with figures for the total rainfall each hour, as well as daily rainfall totals.

In order to get accurate readings, weather stations recording rainfall need to be sited away from buildings, walls, trees or other landscape features that might shelter them from the rain.

Measuring wind speed

The wind speed is measured using an anemometer. The wind catches the cups of the anemometer and makes them turn. This turning generates an electric current in an electrical generator connected to the anemometer. The data logger continually measures the electric current generated and sends this data to the Met Office, where PC software is used to interpret it as wind speeds.

Anemometers should be sited at least 300 metres from large buildings or trees, since these can disrupt the air flow to the anemometer and affect readings.

Checking the equipment

Weather stations need to be checked regularly to ensure that the measurements they provide are accurate. Each weather station in the network is checked weekly by a human observer so that any failures can be corrected quickly, before the data is affected. All the sensors and computer equipment are checked manually every 6 months.

Using ICT in weather stations

Although the technology used in weather stations is expensive, the weather stations are cheap to run. Only a few staff are needed to make the necessary regular checks, so the salary bill is low.

ICT enables the weather stations across the UK to collect more detailed data more accurately than humans could. The data is sent directly to the Met Office so that the central records are always right up to date.

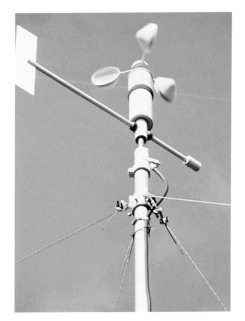

Rain gauge

Anemometer

Recording the weather

1 The tipping bucket rain gauge measures the amount of rain that falls in a day. What other information can it give?

2 Tipping bucket rain gauges, anemometers and thermometers all need to be positioned carefully. Why?

3 Weather stations in towns and cities are more difficult to set up, because 'human factors' affect the readings.

What could these 'human factors' be?

Consider:

- The effect on thermometers of electrical cables, buildings and other man-made structures and systems.
- The effect of buildings on anemometers.
- The effects of human actions, e.g. litter and vandalism.

4 Why do the Met Office only accept data from weather stations set up following their guidelines?

Weather forecasting

1 Use a presentation package to present a TV weather report on a moving weather chart.

Draw icons for the different types of weather, e.g. snow, rain and sunshine. Scan these pictures and use a graphics package to make them look professional.

Your forecast should not be longer than 2 minutes.

2 Keep data on the weather in your area over one week.

- Produce a report on your results.
- Present your results in graphs.
- Comment upon how useful your data is in helping you predict what the local weather will be in the future.
- Suggest ways of making your findings/predictions more effective.
- Describe any problems you encountered with collecting the data and predicting the weather.

3 Use the Internet to investigate the non-scientific methods people have used to forecast the weather in the past. For example, 'Red sky at night' means the weather will …

Write a report of your findings.

4 Write a report for your headteacher explaining why a school is not necessarily a good place for a voluntary weather station.

The police force

ICT can help the police catch criminals and can help to keep police officers safe in dangerous situations. Using ICT the police can collect and analyse large amounts of data on crimes and events all over the country and the world. Some of this data is stored in databases used only in the local police station, but most is stored on national databases.

This data can be used to help in catching criminals and also in planning the numbers of police officers needed in different areas. Some of the new technological devices that the police use to collect data are described later in this unit.

In this unit you will:

- learn how the police use technology to fight crime
- investigate the difference between data and information
- learn about the Data Protection Act.

The police are always in contact with the main police station – sharing information.

What is data?

16 **Data** is facts that have been gathered together. Data of the same type is usually stored together. For example, a business would store customer names and addresses together in a database.

Computers can process data quickly and easily. For example, from a database of traffic incidents a computer could create a list of the best places to deploy police traffic cars.

For data to be useful you need to know its source – where it has come from. These weights are data: 2.7 kg, 3.4 kg, 3.5 kg, 4.2 kg. If you are told that the source of this data is babies' birth weights, you can start to make sense of it – it has been put in context. Data with a source or a context is called information.

Data/information matching

1 Match each group of data with a possible source from the list below.

Group 1	Group 2	Group 3
8:00	8:55	30 min
8:35	9:05	60 min
9:10	9:55	90 min
9:40	10:45	
10:20	11:40	
11:15	12:45	

Group 4	Group 5
28th March	£9.99
20th April	£19.98
12th December	£39.96
12th July	£79.92
20th December	£159.84
9th November	£319.68

Sources:

Bus arrival times

Video running lengths

Prices of goods in shop

Bank holiday dates

School timetable

Audio tape lengths

Television programme schedule

Times for sports matches

Important dates in history

Birthdays

Cooking times for vegetables, fish and meat

A sequence of numbers

2 How easy was it to match the sources with the data groups?

3 What questions did you have to answer for yourself in matching the data to a source?

4 How easy would it be to work out what the data groups were about without the list of sources?

Using data to solve crime

For years police forces have used eye witnesses and fingerprinting to help identify criminals. More recently closed circuit television (CCTV) cameras have been installed in many banks, shops, offices and town centre streets. These record any incidents on film, which the police can use to identify suspects. To fool the cameras and eye witnesses, criminals often wear disguises. However, using new computer technology the police are developing a technique that can identify a suspect through a disguise.

Each face has its own unique bone structure, which determines what that person looks like. By taking measurements of a person's face and the distances between the different facial features, the police can create a map or 'facial fingerprint', which no disguise can hide.

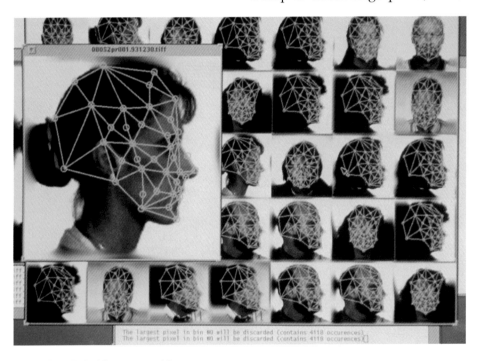

The digital face recognition program works by comparing the relative distances and directions between specific points on a person's head. The grid used here is comparing specific female points.

The facial fingerprint is stored on computer as a series of numbers which detail all the important features of the face. If a crime is filmed on CCTV, similar measurements of facial features can be taken from the film. The computer can check these against the facial fingerprints it has already stored. Once a match is found the computer can then access other information it holds on the suspect, such as name, age and address.

In police trials the facial fingerprinting system has been very effective in identifying criminals whose faces are already on file. It was used in the policing of football hooligans during the Euro2000 competition and is being recommended as an effective way of identifying known troublemakers in large crowds.

Protecting police officers

Police officers often have to go into dangerous situations, for example in riots and fights, and in arresting suspected criminals. The more information they have about such situations, the better they can plan the protection they will need.

To compile this information, all incidents where there is a physical attack or defence are written up in a report. The report says where the incident occurred, who an attack was aimed at, and the method or weapon required to deal with it. The police log this information in their local database and also in a nationwide study.

This kind of data identifies the situations the police are most likely to face on duty. Police officers can then be trained to deal with such situations effectively. Sometimes the data also indicates that new methods or weapons are needed to deal with certain kinds of incident.

New technology

The radar torch is just one example of a technological development that can provide data for police in difficult situations.

The torch sends out a narrow microwave beam that can penetrate walls and return data about things on the other side. The data is fed into a computer, which analyses it and displays a bar chart on the screen.

Data about incidents is recorded and then analysed to help plan policing.

If there is someone on the other side of the wall, the bars in the chart light up and rise and fall as the person breathes in and out. If the person moves, all the bars in the chart light up.

This provides useful information in hostage situations or where intruders are being tracked. The technology is cheap and effective and is likely to be used more widely in future.

How police use data

1 Why do the police record information on violent incidents?

2 The police record information about where incidents occur. How do you think they could use this information when:

   a recruiting officers

   b positioning police cars in towns and cities

   c organising normal working, overtime and holiday working for police officers?

3 How might key dates in the year such as:

   • New Year's Day

   • Christmas Day

   • Cup Final Day

   affect police planning?

Speed cameras

Over the past few years speed cameras have become a common sight by the sides of roads. These capture data on cars that exceed the speed limit, so the police can prosecute the driver. They are an effective way of keeping drivers' speeds down, which helps to reduce the number of accidents, injuries and deaths on the roads.

Speed cameras use a radar system to measure a car's speed. If a car is speeding it is photographed twice. The camera also captures a block of data on the car and prints this on the photograph. All this information provides the evidence that the car was breaking the speed limit.

Interpreting the data block

The camera takes two photographs of the car 0.7 seconds apart. These photographs show how the car has moved relative to a series of lines painted on the road. The police use the markings to calculate the car's speed. This is called a secondary check, as it checks that the camera has accurately identified that the car was speeding. It is an important part of the police evidence if the case comes to court.

Speed cameras are also called Gatso cameras, named after their inventor, Maus Gatsonides.

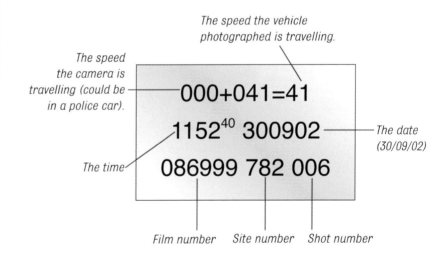

The speed the vehicle photographed is travelling.

The speed the camera is travelling (could be in a police car).

$$000+041=41$$

$$1152^{40} \ 300902$$

The date (30/09/02)

The time

$$086999 \ 782 \ 006$$

Film number   Site number   Shot number

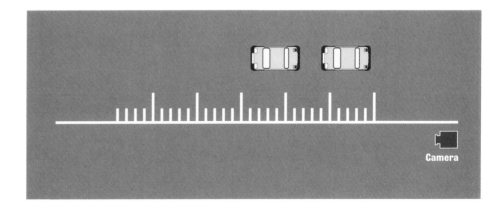

Camera

The spacing between these lines depends on the maximum speed permitted in that area. So the spacing of the lines in a 60mph speed limit is different to the spacing in a 30mph limit.

Look at the diagram of a car's position 0.7 seconds apart in a 30mph

speed limit area. If you look at where the back wheel of the car is in the first position and then compare it with the second position, you will see that the car has moved approximately 8 marks forward. Each mark represents 5mph, so the car was travelling at about 8 x 5 = 40mph, which is over the speed limit for this area.

Speed camera data

1 Look at the data blocks from a Gatso camera and the diagram of the three cars at the first and second photographs.

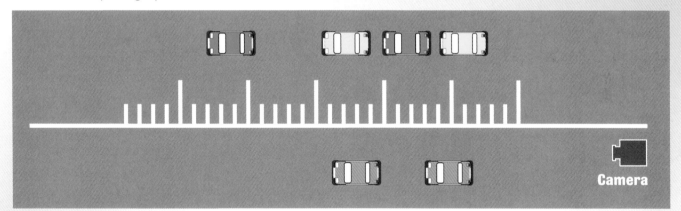

Camera

000+055=55	000+065=65	000+035=35
1159⁴⁰ 300902	1250⁴⁰ 300902	1235⁴⁰ 300902
086999 782 007	086999 782 009	086999 782 011

Match each car to its data block.

2 The speed limit in question 1 was 40mph. Which car should not have been photographed?

3 As well as the evidence in the data block, what data does the photograph show that enables the police to identify the car? Does this evidence always identify the driver? Explain.

4 Why are the secondary check markings needed?

5 Why are the time and date of the photograph important if the police take the evidence from the Gatso camera to court?

FACT FILE
The Data Protection Act, 1984

All companies and organisations that hold personal data about individuals, whether on paper or on computer, must follow the rules laid down in the Data Protection Act.

The Data Protection Act prevents data about an individual being used unless that person has given permission. The Act states that any person or business using personal data must:

- Process any data fairly and lawfully.
- Keep the data only as long as is necessary.
- Keep the data secure so no unauthorised persons can read it.
- Ensure that the data held is accurate and up-to-date.
- Ensure that any data collected is relevant for the purpose and not excessive.

People have the right to view any data held about them, except data held by the police for use in:

- The prevention or detection of crime.
- The apprehension or prosecution of offenders.

Under the Data Protection Act, every organisation holding data must:

- Ensure that data cannot be given out without permission.
- Ensure that the data held is not lost or destroyed accidentally.
- Ensure that records are accurate.

Banks hold information on people's spending and saving habits.

Utility companies hold personal information on their customers.

e-commerce allows companies to collect data on their customers.

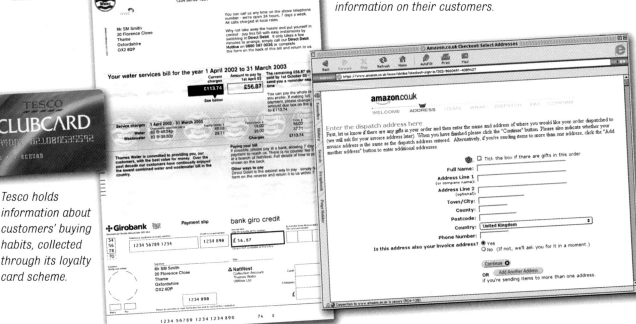

Tesco holds information about customers' buying habits, collected through its loyalty card scheme.

Protecting data

1 Think about five situations where you or your family have given details about yourselves. What information did you give and why?

2 Why do some people object to giving information about themselves?

3 If there was no Data Protection Act, how could some companies misuse personal data?

4 Read these statements.

'Giving data about yourself gives other people power over you. The more data you give, the more businesses and governments can control your lives.'

'The more data we give out, the easier it is for businesses and governments to provide us with the things we need and want.'

Do you agree with either of these statements?
Explain your answer fully.

The Data Protection Act

1 Look at a range of business websites and identify the types of personal data that they might keep about their customers.

2 Find out more about the Data Protection Act.

Write an article for a local newspaper, setting out the main reasons that we need the Act and what it means for businesses that hold personal information about people.

Use a desktop publishing package to set out your article following the template below.

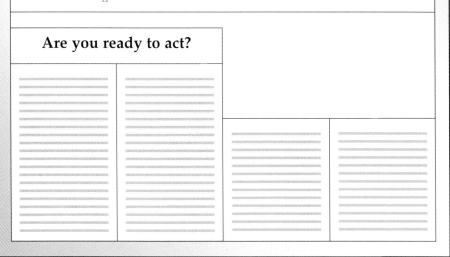

The importance of the Data Protection Act

Are you ready to act?

The Principles of the Data Protection Act prevent misuse of personal information.

Section A

Project 1

Homes of the future

In this project you will:

- use the Internet to find information about homes in the past and what they may be like in the future.
- make a presentation to illustrate the differences between homes from three different times or create a cartoon strip about a time traveller's reactions to these differences.

Hardware and software

	Essential	Useful
Software	Internet browser DTP package presentation package	image manipulation package
Hardware		colour printer digital camera scanner

The project

Choose one of the tasks below. Work in a group of no more than four.

Task 1 Cartoon strip

Create a cartoon strip showing the reactions of a time traveller from the 1950s, who visits homes in the 2000s and 2050s.

Manipulate pictures from the past for use in your strip.

Some of the issues you could deal with are:

- The character's inability to use some modern and future kitchen appliances.
- The character's surprise at the level of automation now and in the future.
- The character's thoughts about the different developments.
- What the character might like to take back to 1950 and which appliances she or he is not impressed with.

Key words for your Internet search are:

- Smart homes
- Future homes
- Homes of the 1950s
- The cool years

Task 2 A presentation on changes in technology

Create a presentation illustrating changes in technology from the 1930s to the present day.

Consider any of these areas of technological change:

- Space travel
- Cars
- Home appliances
- Cinema and film
- Computers

Key phrases to use in your Internet search are:

The history of ...

Project tasks

- Identify suitable websites and books to research the technology of the past.
- Identify websites with details about the future.
- Draw up a draft script based on the resources you have found.
- Storyboard your cartoon or presentation ideas.
- Design your cartoon character using an image manipulation package.
- Divide the different jobs between the members of your group.
- Set a time limit for completing each stage or task.

As you work on your project:

- Make good use of the notes or resources you have collected.
- Manipulate your photo images to show the areas you are interested in to best effect.
- Create and print draft versions.
- Show your ideas to the class. Record any criticisms and make suitable changes.

When your project is completed:

- Present it to your teacher.
- Evaluate your work, using the prompts on page 190.

Section A

Project 2

An Internet guide

In this project you will:
- create a booklet for your school entitled .... School's Guide to the Internet.
- market and sell your booklet to raise money for charity, recording all the details of costs and profit in a spreadsheet.

Hardware and software

	Essential	Useful
Software	word processing package DTP package spreadsheet package	money manager
Hardware		colour printer

The project

Work in a group of no more than four.

Form a production team and create a guide to the internet – an A5 size booklet featuring websites of interest to students. You will need to classify the websites under headings, and rate them according to different criteria. Each website entry should include a short review of the site.

You can design advertisements to market and sell the guide to raise money for charity. You will need to keep accurate records of all your costs and profit.

Keywords and websites that may be helpful are:

- http://www.pbs.org/uti/ – A general guide for beginners
- http://www.ukindex.co.uk/begin0.html – Suitable for lots of internet resources.
- http://www.learnthenet.com/english/index.html – Useful general site

Project tasks

- Survey students to find out which types of website they are interested in.
- Prepare a list of categories the guide will cover.
- Identify suitable websites to include in each category.
- Use rough sketches of the booklet to decide on design and layout, colours, etc.
- Decide on a word limit for the website reviews.
- Divide the different jobs between the members of your group.
- Set a time limit for completing each stage or task.

As you work on your project:

- Keep a master file of all your research notes.
- Have regular meetings to discuss the design and layout of the booklet.
- Take minutes of all meetings. Type them up in a word processing package and save them in the master file.
- Print draft copies of your booklet. Suggest changes that would improve it.
- Show your booklet to the class. Record any criticisms and make suitable changes.
- Record the cost of creating your booklets in a spreadsheet.
- Create advertising posters, letters to parents and advertising leaflets for the guide.
- Record all the final details of costs (including marketing costs) and profit in a spreadsheet.

When your project is completed:

- Present all your work to your teacher.
- Evaluate your work using the prompts on page 190.

Safety and security

In this project you will:

- consider issues of security and safety around your school.
- use the Internet to investigate new technologies that could be helpful in improving school security and safety.

Hardware and software

	Essential	Useful
Software	web browser word processing package	image manipulation package DTP package
Hardware	digital camera	colour printer scanner

The project

Work in a group of no more than four.

Consider safety and security issues around your school.

Create a display board to show the issues you have identified.

Write a report for your headteacher and the local police force, using a word processor. Suggest solutions to the problems you have identified around the school. Your report should describe how technology could be used to solve the problem and to enable the police to identify persistent offenders.

Use the Internet to investigate different solutions to your problems.

Key words and phrases for your Internet search are:

- Sleeping policeman
- Gatso camera
- Trevelo camera
- Vandalism in schools
- Crime in schools
- Making schools safer

Project tasks

- Make a map of the school, identifying areas of concern.
- Use a digital camera to take photographs that illustrate the problems you have identified.
- Identify suitable websites and books for your research.
- Plan your display, based on the resources you have.
- Plan what you will include in your report.
- Divide the different jobs between the members of your group.
- Set a time limit for completing each stage or task.

As you work on your project:

- Make good use of the notes or resources you have collected.
- Have regular meetings to discuss the design and layout of your display and your report.
- Manipulate your photo images to show the areas you are interested in to best effect.
- Create and print draft versions. Suggest improvements you could make.
- Show your ideas to the class. Record any criticisms and make suitable changes.

When your project is completed:

- Present your display and report to your teacher or the class.
- Evaluate your work using the prompts on page 190.

ICT skills

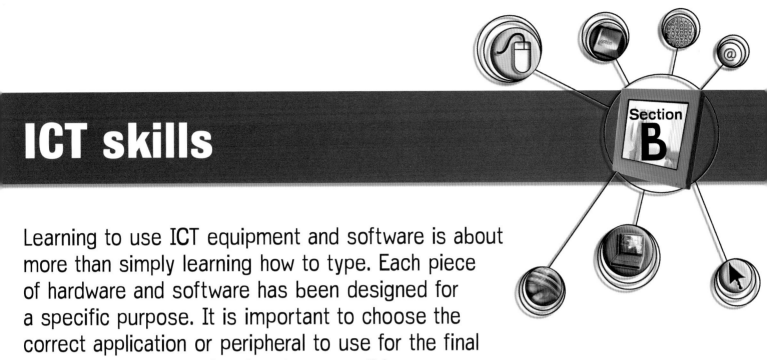

Learning to use ICT equipment and software is about more than simply learning how to type. Each piece of hardware and software has been designed for a specific purpose. It is important to choose the correct application or peripheral to use for the final product to be as professional as possible.

Basic word processing

A word processor is a software program for creating documents. Learning about the basic features of a word processor will help you to understand how many of the applications used on a PC are organised. All word processing packages have similar features.

Understanding applications

The most common PC operating system is Microsoft® Windows®. All the Windows applications are designed in a similar way. This makes them easy to use and understand, even when the software packages are designed to perform different tasks or are made by different companies.

For all Windows applications, including word processors, the screen will show:

● the main title bar

● the menu bars

● the toolbars

● the main display area.

In this unit you will:

● begin to use Microsoft® Word

● use a toolbar and toolbar text

● use menus in a word processor

● learn how to use the help screens in a word processor.

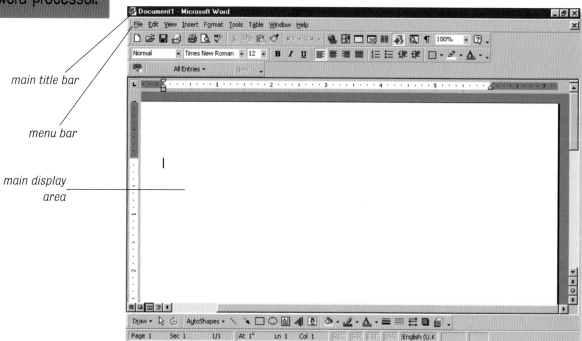

main title bar

menu bar

main display area

The main title bar

This tells you about the document and package being used.

 Document1 - Microsoft Word

In most *Windows* applications the icon for the package you are working in is displayed on the left of the title bar. Next comes the name of the file you are working on, and then the full name of the package.

If the file name is Document, Untitled or another general name, it is likely that the file has not been saved. In this case save the file as soon as possible, as unsaved work may be lost if you make a mistake or your computer stops working.

The file name will then appear on the title bar.

The icons on the right of the title bar allow you to:

- minimise the screen so that you can see the desktop without shutting down your document

- maximise the screen, so that the document displayed fills the whole screen

Saving a document

To save your file:

↗ Click on **File** on the menu bar.

↗ Click on **Save As**... Type the name for your file in the blank box next to **File name:**

↗ Click on **OK**.

 maximise   *minimise*   *exit*

- exit the program.

Experiment with these icons to see how they work.

If you use the exit icon to exit the program, you will usually be prompted to save your work if you have not already done so.

Health and safety

Investigate the health and safety implications of using a word processor for long periods of time.

The menu bar

In most *Windows* applications there is only one menu bar and it is always shown on the screen. The menu bar may have several options, but it is always likely to include these four: **File**, **Edit**, **View** and **Help**.

Clicking on the words with the mouse displays menus which will include the following options.

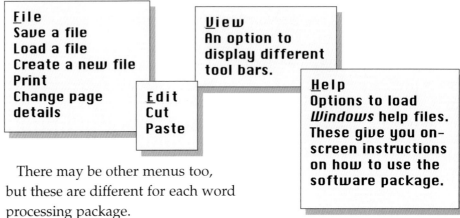

There may be other menus too, but these are different for each word processing package.

Toolbars

Every tool or action available is in a menu list. However, it can be difficult to remember where things are in the lists. The toolbars make things quicker – you just click on a button to use a tool.

There are many different toolbars, depending on the package you use. If the toolbar you need is not shown on screen you need to choose it from the toolbar menu. To do this click on **View** and then **Toolbars** and then select a suitable toolbar.

The toolbar buttons use icons. If you float your mouse cursor over a toolbar button the toolbar text for that button will appear in a few seconds. This gives a brief description of what the button does.

The File menu box from Word.

Toolbar text appears if you float the mouse cursor over a toolbar button B.

Windows help

If you do not know how to do something in your word processor, you can use the **Help** menu. This will offer you different ways to find out what you need to know. The most common options are:

- an assistant
- help pages
- links to an Internet site.

An assistant

Many different *Windows* applications use assistants to help users find their way around a package. Often you can type questions for the assistant and the assistant will find all the topics that it thinks are relevant. These are always a good place to start searching, as the assistant will often bring up answers to frequently asked questions.

Help pages

If your question or problem is more specific you can go into the help contents pages or the index and search for the answers to a question. This method is likely to be most useful in finding answers, but only if you know **key words** relating to the task you are trying to perform.

Links to an Internet site

Internet links should be the last place you look for help. These links are often written by teachers or other users, who wish to suggest easy ways of remembering or performing a task. However, pages can often be slow to load and it may be difficult to find the exact answer to a specific question.

The main display or work area

This area is where you manipulate text or graphics and create documents or images. In all packages, including word processors, there are some basic skills to learn.

Typing text

In *Windows* applications there is usually a flashing or blinking cursor. The cursor often looks like a bold vertical line. It indicates where text will be entered on the page if you type using the keyboard. Generally, if the cursor is not visible or blinking, you cannot enter text.

As you type, the cursor will automatically move to the next line when you reach the end of the previous one. This is called word wrap.

To start a new paragraph you need to use the Return key.

Copying text

It is useful to be able to copy passages in a word processor or spreadsheet, so you can repeat sections or move text around easily.

Copy and paste

↗ Highlight the text you want to copy. Use the mouse to position the flashing cursor in front or at the end of the word or paragraph to copy. Hold down the left mouse button and drag the mouse to the start or end of the section. The words should change to being white in a coloured box.

↗ Once the text is highlighted click on **Edit** and then **Copy**. The text is copied and placed on the clipboard – an area which holds information.

↗ Now position the flashing cursor where you want to insert the text.

↗ Click on **Edit** and then **Paste**. The text you copied is then taken from the clipboard and inserted on the page.

Cut and paste

➔ First highlight the text you want to copy, as for copy and paste.

➔ Once the text is highlighted click on **Edit** and then **Cut**. The text is cut from the screen, but is copied and placed on the clipboard.

➔ Now position the flashing cursor where you want to insert the text.

➔ Click on **Edit** and then **Paste**. The text you copied is then taken from the clipboard and inserted on the page.

You can also use the copy, cut and paste buttons from the toolbar for these tasks. Follow the same process, using the buttons instead of the menu options.

 copy button   *cut button*   *paste button*

● *Changing text appearance*

You can change the size and colour of the text, and the text font. First highlight the text and then use the toolbar to make the changes.

The formating tool bar.

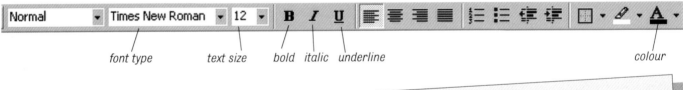

font type   text size   bold italic underline   colour

Arial font 10 point in red

Comic Sans MS font 14 point in orange

Times New Roman font 11 point Bold in black

Gill Sans font 12 point Italic in black

Palatino font 24 point in black

Helvetica font 14 point in green

Wingdings 12 point black ☺ℳ◆◆ℳ▢•

Zapf dingbats 16 point blue ✳❀❑❄❄❉
■✳✪❀▼▲✏✂✡♣♠

● *Justifying and aligning text*

You can position text on the page in different ways.

> **Centred** – the text is placed at an equal distance from the left and right margins.
>
> **Left justified** – the text lines up with the left margin.
>
> **Right justified** – the text lines up with the right margin.
>
> **Fully justified** – the text is spaced to line up with both the left and right margins. This text is fully justified. This text is fully justified. This text is fully justified. This text is fully justified. This

Centred text button

Left justified text button

Right justified text button

Fully justified text button

Justifying text

↗ Use the appropriate buttons on your toolbar.

↗ Or click on **Format** then **Paragraph** and then change the settings of the alignment box.

Word processing skills

1 What are the main differences between the menu bar and the toolbars?

2 Draw the main features which can be seen in any *Windows* application. Label each part and briefly describe their purpose.

3 Explain the different between Cut and Copy.

4 Which help option would you select:

- If you had searched the help screens and used the assistant but found no answers to your questions?

- If this was your first attempt at finding the answer to your question?

- If you had a very specific question which was not answered by the assistant?

5 Look at the fonts examples on page 80.

For what purpose or document might you use each font?

6 Design your own font on paper.

Try incorporating stars, flowers or pebbles in the design.

What could you use each of your designs for?

Computer guide

Create step-by-step guides for new computer users, giving basic instructions on how to:

- display the drawing toolbar

- hide the drawing toolbar

- change the size of text on a page

- change the alignment of text on a page

- find the spelling and grammar functions on the toolbar and in the menu options.

Remember you may need to explain what a toolbar or menu bar is in your descriptions.

13 More word processing

A word processor is a software program for creating documents. These documents can be stored on disk as files, retrieved, edited, formatted and then printed.

The advantage of using a word processor is that you can re-load your files and change documents at a later date, or import your text into other applications.

One of the most popular word processing applications is Microsoft *Word®*. The instructions in this unit are for *Word*, but you will find similar tools available in all word processors.

Organising text

A long piece of text can be quite daunting. You can use the following ideas to organise your text and make it easier to read.

In this unit you will:
- learn more advanced word processing skills
- combine information from different sources into your documents.

Bullet points
- Highlight the text for the list and click the Bullets button on the toolbar. The word processor will automatically bullet your list.
- If your toolbar is not displayed, click on **Format** and then **Bullets and Numbering**.

Using bullets

> **Computer components**
> - Keyboard
> - Mouse
> - Screen
> - Printer

Numbered lists
- Highlight the text for the list and click the Numbering button on the toolbar. The word processor will automatically number your list.
- If your toolbar is not displayed, click on **Format** and then **Bullets and Numbering**.

Using numbering

> **Start-up procedure**
> 1. Switch on main power button
> 2. Switch on box power
> 3. Switch on monitor
> 4. Wait for operating system to load

A long piece of text can be quite daunting...

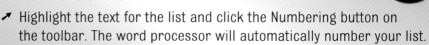

Indenting text

↗ To move a block of text away from the left margin, highlight it and click the Increase Indent button on the toolbar.

↗ To move a block of text back towards the margin, click the Decrease Indent button on the toolbar.

↗ If your toolbar is not displayed, click on **Format** then **Paragraph** and type in the indent required.

Tables

↗ • If you are using Office 97, click on **Table** then **Insert Table**.

• For Office 2000 click on **Table** then **Insert** and then **Table**.

• For XP click on **Table** then **Insert** then **Table**.

↗ In the dialogue box that appears, choose the numbers of rows and columns you need. Think carefully how many you will need.

↗ To add a new row:

Add new rows at the bottom of a table by moving your cursor to the bottom right cell and pressing the Tab key.

Or

• In Office 97 click on **Table**, then **Insert rows**.

• In Office 2000 click on Table, then Insert and the option for rows.

• For XP, select a cell or row next to where you would like to add the new row. Click on **Table** and then use the options given to choose where the new row should be inserted.

↗ To insert a new column:

• For Office 97 highlight the column to the left of where you wish to insert the new column. Click on **Table**, then **Insert columns**.

• For Office 2000 highlight a cell to the left of where you wish to insert the new column and click on **Table**, then **Insert** and the option for columns.

• For XP, select a cell or column next to where you would like to add the new column. Click on **Table** and then use the options given to choose where the new column should be inserted.

↗ Print your table with or without gridlines by clicking the Outside Border button or by clicking on **Format** and then **Borders and Shading** and choosing the option you prefer.

Shading and border option.

Headers and footers

For a multi-page document, you can automatically display information to identify the document on each page.

In your headers and footers you might like to include:

- page numbers
- file name
- author
- date prepared.

Information at the top of each page is called a header.

Information at the bottom of each page is called a footer.

Inserting headers and footers

↗ To insert headers and footers click on **View** and then **Header and footer**. A new toolbar should appear. Float your cursor over the toolbar to reveal the text explaining what each button does.

Livening up your document

WordArt

WordArt allows you to create interesting text effects to make a word stand out from the page, usually in headings.

Using *WordArt*

↗ To use *WordArt* you need to have the drawing toolbar selected. To get this, click on **View**, then **Toolbars**, then **Drawing**.

↗ Select the Insert WordArt button from the toolbar.

↗ Choose a *WordArt* style for the colour and shape of the heading.

↗ Type in the text you require.

↗ Change the appearance of your text using the tools on the *WordArt* toolbar. This appears automatically when you insert *WordArt*.

Shapes, arrows and 3D

The drawing toolbar contains other features, such as the shape tool, arrows and possibly a 3D setting.

You can use these features to draw attention to items of interest.

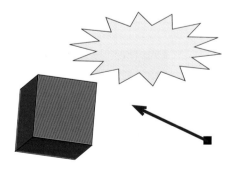

Screen dumps

You can use screen dumping in all *Windows* applications. It inserts a picture of the screen in your document.

A screen dump is useful when you are creating a user manual for a program, or demonstrating how to perform a particular task. In these situations you may want to include information that appears on your computer screen, for example the menu options.

Making a screen dump

↗ First bring up the screen image you want.

↗ Press the 'Print Screen' key on the keyboard (this may be abbreviated, e.g. to Prt Sc). The screen image is now on the clipboard.

↗ Position your cursor in the document where you want the image. Now either use the Paste button or click on **Edit** then **Paste**.

↗ Change the position or size of your image if necessary.

If you import the image into a graphics package before inserting it you can crop and edit the image to include only the parts that you want.

Creating business documents

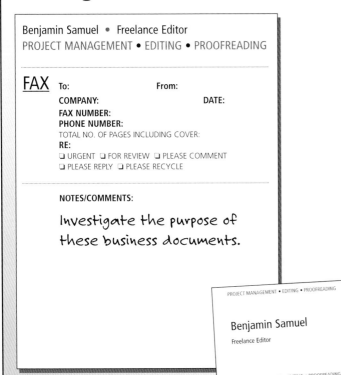

Benjamin Samuel • Freelance Editor
PROJECT MANAGEMENT • EDITING • PROOFREADING

FAX To: From:
COMPANY: DATE:
FAX NUMBER:
PHONE NUMBER:
TOTAL NO. OF PAGES INCLUDING COVER:
RE:
❏ URGENT ❏ FOR REVIEW ❏ PLEASE COMMENT
❏ PLEASE REPLY ❏ PLEASE RECYCLE

NOTES/COMMENTS:

Investigate the purpose of these business documents.

PROJECT MANAGEMENT • EDITING • PROOFREADING

Benjamin Samuel
Freelance Editor

PROJECT MANAGEMENT • EDITING • PROOFREADING

Create a series of business documents, using the features provided in *Word*.

Some ideas are:

- business card
- letterhead
- fax header
- memo
- invoice.

Remember that the audience for these documents is the customers of business professionals. Therefore the documents must be high quality and well presented, without spelling errors and with careful thought to the images used in the business logo.

Benjamin Samuel • Freelance Editor
PROJECT MANAGEMENT • EDITING • PROOFREADING

Ravinder Singh
Dodo Publishing Ltd
41 High Street
Busytown
BS3 1PQ

Dear Mr Singh,

Benjamin Samuel • Freelance Editor
PROJECT MANAGEMENT • EDITING • PROOFREADING

\<First Name\> \< Surname\>
\<Company name\>
\<Street name\>
\<Town / City\>
\<Postcode\>

Dear \<Mr / Miss / Mrs\> \<Surname\>

Mail merge

Often businesses wish to send the same letter to many different people. Each person has a different name and address, so each letter has to have a different set of information. Mail merge allows you to create one main document and print it with many different names and addresses, rather than having to type the document many times.

If you are using a more recent version of Word than Word 2000, there is an easy to follow Wizard that will take you through each stage of mail merge.

Mail merge in XP

↗ Click on **Tools** then **Letters and Mailings** and select the Mail merge wizard.

↗ Work through the task pane to the right of the screen, following the detailed instructions.

Creating your main document

Mail merge in *Word* 97 or 2000

↗ Type your letter or main document.

↗ Click on **Tools** then **Mail Merge**. Select **Create**.

↗ Choose **Form Letters.**

↗ You are then asked if you wish to use the active window or new main document.

The active window is the one that contains your created letter. Select this option.

Creating the data source

 Word can use records held in an **Excel**® or **Access**® format to access data about the people you wish to send this letter to.

You can also type in the names and details of these people in *Word*. Follow the instructions at the top of page 87.

Preparing mail merge data

↗ Select **Get Data**.

↗ Choose **Create data source**.

↗ Add and remove the headings for the different data you will use in your letter.

For example, in a personal letter you would not include the person's job title in the address. Select the job title heading and choose **Remove field name**.

To include data, type the heading name into the Field name box and select **Add field name**.

↗ Save the data, to a file. You may wish to use this list at a later date.

↗ Select **Edit data source** and enter your data on the people the letter is to be sent to, selecting **Add New** after each record.

When you have finished entering the data click on **OK**.

Link your data and letter

Your data and your letter are still two separate items. The software does not know where to enter the data you have typed in.

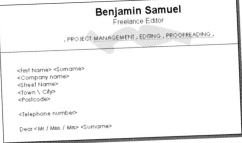

Linking the data and the document

↗ A bar should have appeared at the top of your *Word* screen, with a button Insert Merge Fields. Select this and it shows you a list of all the headings you kept earlier in the process.

↗ Work through your document to place the merge fields in the appropriate places. Position the cursor where you wish to insert the information. Click on the Insert Merge Field button.

↗ Select the field you want to put into your letter at the point where the cursor is flashing. Remember to insert the correct spacing and punctuation between fields.

↗ When you have finished, return to the Mail Merge option and select Merge.

In the dialogue box that appears, make sure you have chosen Merge to: New Document, and click on the Merge button.

When you merge the two together, the software will automatically replace the fields with the data you put into your data source, personalising each copy of your standard letter.

↗ Save your file with an appropriate name before printing your letters.

Using Outline view

This useful feature can be accessed by selecting Outline from the **View** menu.

Outline view allows you to view the structure of the whole document, without having to read through it all. You can also use it to move sections of text around in long or complex documents, without having to cut and paste.

This is the start of an essay about the state of UK railways.

Railways 'compare badly with Europe'
   ◇ **BY GISELA ENGLISH**

   ◇ **Introduction**
      □ *Britain's train system is the worst in Europe, according to railway experts. Countries such as France and Germany have better high-speed inter-city services, although their regional and local services are poor compared with Britain.*

   ◇ **The history of Britain's train system**
      ◇ *Although most exponents agree that the British system has its good points, they have to admit that they are unlikely to hear the praise offered by the French for their high speed TGV trains.*
      □
   ~~Comparing Britain's trains with those in Europe~~

In this example Outline view shows the essay title, the author, and the main section headings, with the first line of each section shown for each heading. This view gives you a good idea of what the essay is about, without reading the whole document.

The text is set out in steps. The further to the right each piece of text is, the less important it is in the structure of the document. You can use the numbered buttons on the tool bar to hide different parts of the document. Button 1 shows just the main heading – the title of the essay (furthest to the left on the screen). Button 2 shows the author's name as well as the title. Button 3 shows the main section headings. This is useful, especially in long documents or projects, when you want to check things are in the correct order without reading through the whole document.

The + and – signs

A + sign next to a heading shows that this section has text linked to it.

In the example the section headed 'Introduction' has text. If you move the section heading by dragging the plus (+) sign with the mouse, the text will move with it.

A minus (–) sign shows that there are no subheadings or subsections of text in this section. There may be other headings on the same level in the document.

Moving sections

You can use the promote and demote arrows to move text and headings up or down in the order of importance.

This is useful if you wish to make text belong to a heading. Once text belongs to a heading you can use the up and down arrows to move this heading and its text to a different place in the document, without cutting or pasting.

Word processors

1 Describe 10 features that you would find in a typical word processing package. Copy and fill in this table, ranking the features from 1 to 5 (1 being the highest) under these headings.

Feature	Usefulness	Importance for your work	Difficulty of performing the task	Impact

Compare your table with a friend's. Do you both use the same features?

2 What sort of features should word processors of tomorrow have?

Describe your ideas and design images for the new toolbar buttons to show clearly what your new function does.

3 List the advantages and disadvantages of using a word processor.

Give some examples of written communications where using a word processor would not be appropriate.

4 Direct mail is the most rapidly increasing form of promotion. Give one advantage it has over television advertising for a business and one disadvantage it has over television advertising for the customer.

The majority of mailshots are read. How do direct mailers persuade us to read them?

Letters and emails

1 Compose an email in *Word* to invite a friend to your house for the weekend. Include a graphic and a list of things they should bring with them. Copy and paste your work into an email package.

2 Design a letter that your school could use in a mailshot to persuade local parents to choose your school for their children currently in Year 6.

Choose a font style and size and use bold, italics, bullet points and indents as appropriate.

What database could the school use to mail merge with your letter?

14 Using a desktop publishing package

Desktop publishing (DTP) packages make it easy to create professional quality work on a PC.

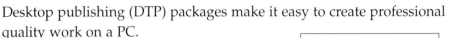

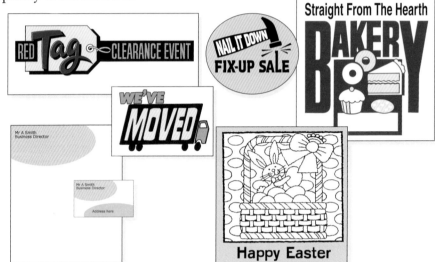

DTP packages

In DTP the elements of a document – text, images, *WordArt*, etc. – are laid out in separate boxes. You can then move these boxes around on the page to find the most effective layout. This makes DTP packages much more flexible than wordprocessors for producing documents.

There are many DTP packages. Microsoft® *Publisher* is the one most schools use. The program contains layouts for different types of document and Wizards – step-by-step guides to help you produce a document to a pre-set format. Some DTP packages have templates for different documents. These are documents with a basic design and layout that users can alter to suit their own needs.

Using Wizards

When you open a new file in *Publisher* you are given the option of using a Wizard. The styles available will be displayed on your screen. Choose the style you want, then follow the step-by-step instructions on screen.

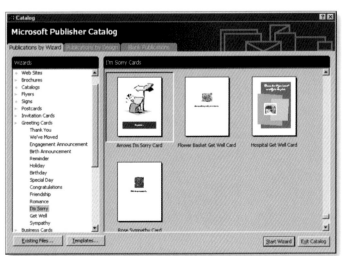

When the document Wizard has finished you can replace any pictures with others by double clicking on the picture you wish to change, then inserting the graphic you have chosen. Or you can right click on the picture and then insert your chosen image.

Inserting graphics

↗ Click on **Insert** and then go to **Picture**. Then choose **Clip Art** to choose from the *ClipArt* provided with the software.

↗ Choose **From File** to import a picture from another file on your computer.

You can import graphics from:

● a *ClipArt* file
● scanned images
● other applications, e.g. Internet, encyclopaedias, etc.
● your own graphics created in another package.

Remember: always check to see if an image has any **copyright** restrictions before you use it in a publication for distribution.

Designing your own document

You may prefer to design your document from scratch instead of using Wizards. This gives you maximum flexibility, but you need to plan carefully.

❏ Who is the audience?

❏ Should it be portrait or landscape?

❏ What is the purpose of the document?

❏ Is it clear in which order you should read the blocks of text? Do you need borders or arrows?

❏ Do all the pages in the document have the same basic design? Too many changes of layout and text fonts can confuse the reader.

❏ What graphics will you use? Are they all relevant? Where will you obtain the graphics? Where will you position them?

❏ What size, colour and style of font will you use for headings? Should they have a border?

❏ What text layout will you use? Columns or blocks?

❏ What size, colour and font will you use for the body text? Will the body text be smaller than the heading? What about sub-headings?

portrait

landscape

14

Changing text colour

↗ Highlight the text with the mouse, then click on **Format** then **Font**. Choose from the colours displayed.

Text researching

1 Find out what serif and sans serif fonts are.
2 Look in newspapers, books and magazines.
  a When are serif fonts used?
  b When are sans serif fonts used?
3 Find out more about the use of serif and sans serif fonts. Are there any basic rules on when you should and should not use each font type?
4 Make a collection of different magazine advertisements and articles. Look at the different page layouts.
  a How does white space contribute to a document?
  b How important is it to place pictures correctly?

Using a Wizard

Create a new document and use the Wizard to make a letterhead for an imaginary business. Use a suitable graphic in your design.

Then create a business card using the same design as your letterhead.

Backgrounds for documents

You can insert images in *Publisher* documents as a backdrop for text. These can be in full colour or you can recolour the picture so it appears less strongly on the page. This is often called a watermark.

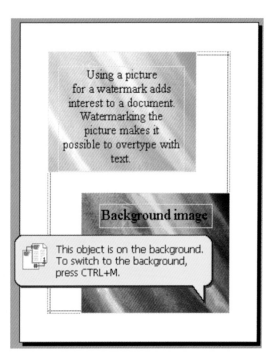

Using a picture for a watermark adds interest to a document. Watermarking the picture makes it possible to overtype with text.

Background image

This object is on the background. To switch to the background, press CTRL+M.

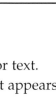

Inserting background images

↗ Click on **View**, then **Go to Background**.

↗ Insert the picture or text you would like as a background or watermark by clicking on **Insert** and then **Picture** and selecting the correct source file.

↗ Click on **View** and then **Go to Foreground** to see your document with the background image in place.

↗ To change the colour of the background picture, click on **View**, then **Go to Background** again. Click on the picture and then click on **Format** then **Recolor Picture**.

↗ To change the background colour of a text box click on **View**, then **Go to Foreground** again. Click on the text box, then click on **Format** then **Fill Color**. You are given a choice of colours, with more available in the **More Colors** menu option.

Altering images

You can change the images in your document so they stand out more, or fit the space available.

In *Publisher*, select the image in your document with the mouse, then click on **Format** and you will find the options **Recolor Picture**, **Scale Picture**, **Crop Picture** and **Shadow**.

- **Recolor Picture** allows you to change the colour of the image, for example from full colour to black and white.

- **Scale Picture** allows you to reduce or increase the size of an image without distorting it.

- **Crop Picture** allows you to trim an image so that only the relevant area is seen.

- **Shadow** places a faint shadow behind the image, so it appears to stand out from the page.

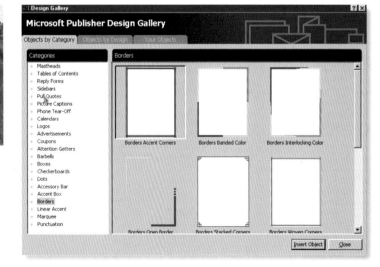

Design gallery

DTP packages have a gallery of borders and graphics for you to use in your documents.

Using the design gallery

↗ Click on **Insert** and then **Design Gallery Object**. A list of object category titles appears on the left. There are pictures showing individual objects within the selected category on the right.

↗ Browse this list to see if any of the items will compliment your chosen design style. When you have chosen one, double click on it, or select it and click on the **Insert Object** button.

Framing text and images

You can add frames around text blocks or images to increase their impact.

Picture framing

To change the way text will appear around a picture:

↗ Select the picture with the mouse, then click on **Format** then **Picture Frame Properties**.

↗ Setting the **Wrap text** around option to **Entire frame** will ensure that no text will appear in the rectangular frame around your picture.

If you prefer text to wrap around the picture itself, select **Picture only** instead.

INTELLIGENT ANIMALS

Adding borders

↗ Click on the image or text box you want to frame with a border.

↗ Click on **Format** then **Line/Border Style** then **More Styles** and select the tab **BorderArt**. This gives you a choice of borders.

Comparing DTP and wordprocessing packages

1 Decide whether you would use a DTP package or a word processor for each of these:

- write a letter
- create a business card
- create a poster
- merge addresses and text documents
- draw a map
- create a birthday invitation
- create a banner
- create an award certificate
- compose an essay

2 Which allows the user to be more creative – a DTP package or a word processor? Explain your answer.

3 List the different functions each package can perform.

4 Some of the items listed in question 1 can be created in either a DTP or word processing package. Which are they?

So why do we need two different packages?

5 Create some A4 posters to help computer users choose the correct package to create their documents.

Creative publishing

1 Experiment with the DTP features described in this unit.

Use the techniques you have learned to create some of these:

- gone to lunch sign
- calendar
- letterhead or compliments slip
- bedroom name tag
- wedding invitation
- poster advertising something for sale.

2 Create a range of cards for:

- birthdays
- congratulations
- anniversaries
- get well soon.

For each card write a brief design specification explaining which special features you have used to create it and why the images, text and layout are suitable for the occasion.

Using a spreadsheet

15

A spreadsheet is a type of computer software. It was originally developed to help accountants make calculations.

Nowadays spreadsheets are used to present data involving numbers, text and charts, and for many different types of calculations. Spreadsheets help to make repetitive tasks involving numbers and calculations quicker and easier.

In this unit you will:

- learn how to manipulate text in a spreadsheet
- use a spreadsheet for calculations
- manage complex decision-making functions.
- create charts to display data.

You can use a spreadsheet for all sorts of tasks, such as keeping track of your finances. Businesses use spreadsheets to predict future sales or other events, based on numerical information such as population growth or Internet usage. They set up the spreadsheet using formulae that will do the same calculations for different sets of data. In this way they can model situations and predict trends.

There are many different spreadsheet packages. The instructions in this chapter are for *Excel*®, from the Microsoft® *Office* suite, but you should be able to carry out the same tasks in most other spreadsheet packages you use.

Finding your way around a spreadsheet

When you first load a spreadsheet you will notice that it is a grid of rows and columns. The columns are usually labelled using letters, starting with A. The rows are numbered from 1.

A typical spreadsheet looks like this:

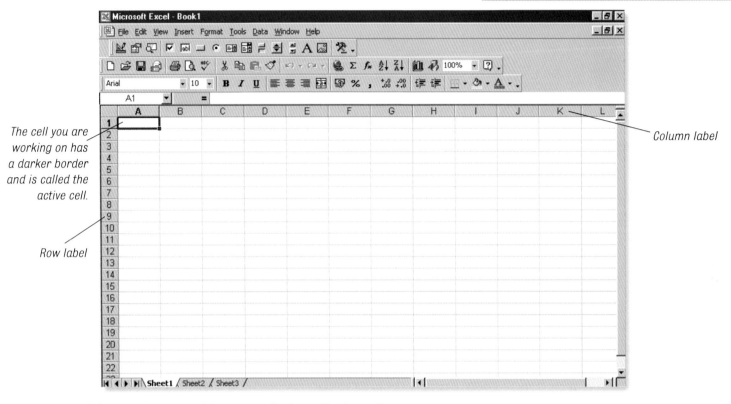

The cell you are working on has a darker border and is called the active cell.

Row label

Column label

Each small box in the spreadsheet is called a cell. The cells are identified by their column and row. For example, cell C6 is the cell in column C row 6.

Information in a spreadsheet is usually set out as a table with column headings. When you create your spreadsheet you can type in text or numbers in any font or size, and change to bold or italic, or centre text, just as you would using a word processor.

The column and row labels, and the borders around the cells, are there to help you add and sort data. They do not usually print out when you print the spreadsheet.

Altering more than one cell

↗ To change the text for more than one cell at a time, highlight the whole area first by holding down the left hand mouse button and dragging. Or you can highlight a whole column at once by clicking on the column heading.

↗ Then change the text style. Your changes will apply to all of the highlighted area.

Merging cells

If the title of your table, or any other piece of text, is too long to fit into one cell, you can merge two or more cells.

Merging cells
↗ Highlight the cells you wish to merge
↗ Click on the Merge and Center button.
Or click on **Format** and then **Cells**, choose **Alignment**, make sure the Merge cells box is ticked, and then click on **OK**.

Wrapping text

If you have a lot of text to fit in one cell you can increase the width of the cell or make it deeper by moving the cursor to the column or row label. You will notice that the cursor changes shape into two smaller arrows. By holding down the left hand mouse button you can drag the cell to any size. This may look strange, especially if you are creating a sheet with text and numbers, because one column or row may be wider than all the rest, or a large column heading may look out of place.

Instead you can wrap text within the cell. This keeps the width of the cell fixed but allows you to type two or more lines of text in the cell. Or you can shrink the text to fit the cell.

Wrap text
↗ Highlight the cell (s).
↗ Click on **Format**, then **Cells**, choose **Alignment**, then choose either **Wrap text** or **Shrink to fit**.

Text orientation

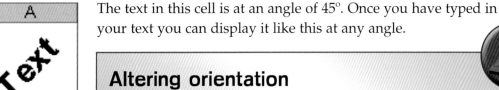

The text in this cell is at an angle of 45°. Once you have typed in your text you can display it like this at any angle.

Altering orientation
↗ Highlight the cells.
↗ Click on **Format** then **Cells**, then **Alignment**, then **Orientation**.
↗ Either type in the angle or use the mouse to move the Text pointer.

Colour and shading

To enhance your table you can fill cells with colour, change the font colour or put borders around some or all of the cells.

Colouring cells

↗ Highlight the cells you want to change.

↗ Use the buttons for border, fill cells and font colour.

 The button to use for adding borders to a table.

↗ Or click on **Format** then **Cells** then either **Patterns, Font** or **Border**.

↗ Or highlight your completed table and then click on **Format** then **AutoFormat** and you will be given a whole range of different styles to choose from.

Understanding cells

1 What is written in cell C2?

2 Which cell or cells are active?

3 Write down the label for a cell where:

- Cells are merged horizontally.
- Cells are merged vertically.
- The text has been orientated at an angle.
- The text has been wrapped.
- A large font size has been used.
- A small font size has been used.
- Cells are filled with colour.

4 What does it mean when you say a cell is active?

5 Row 4 has been enlarged. How was this done?

	A	B	C	D	E
1	Record of personal information				
2	Pupil	Height	Age	Shoe Size	
3	Rebecca				
4	Geraldine				
5	Benjamin				
6	Melanie				
7	Peter				
8	Matthew				
9	Jayne				
10	John				
11	Helen				
12	Stephen				
13	Christopher				

Class of 2000

Sorting text alphabetically

You may wish to keep the text in one column linked to the text in other columns. For example, if you have first and family names, age and gender in three columns, you want to keep the age and gender details alongside the correct names when you sort the names in alphabetical order.

To do this, highlight all the cells and click on **Data** then **Sort**. Then select the criterion you wish to sort by.

Numbers

You can put numbers into a spreadsheet using either the top row of keys beneath the function keys or the numeric keypad to the right of the keyboard. If you are using the numeric keypad make sure that you have the number lock on.

Cell format for numbers

You can format a cell so that it displays the numbers you enter in a standard way.

For example, if you format the cell to display currency and type in 5000, the cell will display this as £5000. Typing 50.00 gives the display £50.00.

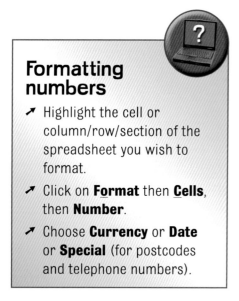

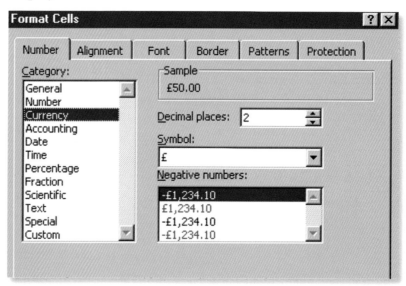

Search and replace

Suppose 300 students' exam results are entered in the spreadsheet, but the name Graham has been typed incorrectly as 'grham' each time. Instead of searching for each 'Graham' in the spreadsheet and correcting them one at a time, you can change the cells into the correct format all at once.

Using edit and replace

↗ Highlight the column you want to search (the column of first names in this example).

↗ Click on **Edit** then **Replace.**

↗ A 'Find what' box appears. Type in what you are searching for (grham in this example).

↗ In the 'Replace with' box type what you want to replace it with (Graham in this example).

↗ Click on **Replace All**. (The program finds all the grhams in the highlighted column and replaces them with Graham.)

Using formulae

Once you have put numbers into the spreadsheet you can do calculations with them by putting in formulae.

If you have a bank account the bank sends you regular statements. The amount in the bank account is calculated by adding the money deposited to any money already in the account, and subtracting the money withdrawn. This gives the formula for the balance:

$$\text{Balance} = \begin{pmatrix} \text{Money in account} \\ \text{at start of month} \end{pmatrix} - \begin{pmatrix} \text{Money} \\ \text{withdrawn} \end{pmatrix} + \begin{pmatrix} \text{Money} \\ \text{deposited} \end{pmatrix}$$

The statement can be created as a spreadsheet using this formula. When the money deposited and withdrawn from the account is entered in the spreadsheet it will automatically calculate the balance in the account.

The formula goes into the cell where you want the result to appear.

A formula can use a combination of numbers and cell references. The most important thing to remember is that formulae must always begin with the equals (=) sign. Without this sign your spreadsheet will not work.

Writing formulae

The formula

$=3+6$

adds 3 and 6.

The formula

$=A2+6$

adds 6 to the value in cell A2.

These are the signs to use in formulae:

/ Divide

* Multiply

+ Add

− Minus

Special functions

You use formulae for short and simple calculations. But you can select more complex functions from the functions menu box. This appears in the top left hand corner of a spreadsheet when you enter the equals (=) sign into a cell.

These functions make calculations easier. For example, the function AVERAGE calculates the mean of a column of numbers.

Some of the most useful functions on the functions menu are:

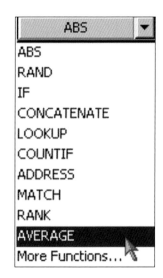

- SUM – This function adds all the numbers in selected cells together without having to use lots of + signs.
- MAX – This function identifies the largest number in a range of cells.
- MIN – This function identifies the lowest number in a range of cells.

Type the function in the cell where you want the result to appear.

Experiment with the other functions listed in the menu. If you have problems use the Help feature in *Excel*.

The functions menu

To use a function from the functions menu, type in:

- ↗ = This tells the computer that you are using a function or formula.
- ↗ The name of the function, e.g. AVERAGE
- ↗ The range of cells to look at, in brackets, e.g. (A1:B2)

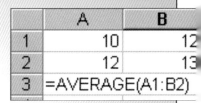

This means the computer should look at the cells in the range A1 to B2, as shown.

So the function will look like this: = AVERAGE(A1:B2)

The IF function

This function allows you to try different data to see what the results would be each time. This is called What If analysis.

For example, for a school trip a teacher has to calculate the price pupils have to pay to cover the costs. The trip can only go ahead if the price is below £35 per head.

	A	B	C	D	E
1	**Trip**				
2					
3	Costs			Income	
4					
5	Bus	1300		Donations	200
6	Total ticket cost	500		Subsidy	300
7	Food	150			
8					
9	**Total Costs**	1950		**Total Income**	500
10		=SUM(B5:B8)			=SUM(E5:E8)
11					
12	**Total left to pay**	1450			
13		=B9-E9			
14	**Number of pupils on trip**	30			
15					
16	**Pupil cost**	48.33			
17		=B11/B13			
18					
19	**Go ahead ?**	Cancel			
20					

The spreadsheet calculates the cost per pupil and displays it in cell B16. The IF statement below is entered into cell B19. It automatically checks whether the trip cost is below £35. If it is, the trip will go ahead and the cell displays the word OK. If not the cell displays the word Cancel.

=IF(B16<35, "OK", "Cancel")

The IF function allows you to put one value in the cell if something is true and another value if it is false. You can link up to seven IF functions in one cell and use very complex IF statements. Experiment with simple ones like the one above first.

The COUNTA function

If you enter the formula =COUNTA(A1:A35) into Cell A36, the spreadsheet counts the number of cells in the column above A36 (from A1 to A35) that have something in them. It shows the answer in cell A36.

This function could be used to count the number of pupils in a class list.

=	says that a formula or function is being used.
IF	the name of the function
(	the start of instructions
	The instruction is 'look at cell B16 and see if the value there is less than 35'
,	the first comma means 'then'
"..."	the word in quotation marks will be shown in the cell. If you use numbers instead of words you don't need the quotation marks.
,	the second comma means 'else', or 'otherwise'.
"..."	In this case show the word Cancel.
)	indicates the end of instructions.

Spreadsheet functions

1 Do you know your 19 times table? Most of us don't.

Using a spreadsheet to construct any multiplication table will help you practise.

Creating the 19 times table

↗ Load the spreadsheet and type 1 in cell A1.

↗ You need to enter a formula in B1.

Type = A1*19 (multiply A1 by 19) and press Enter.

19 should appear in cell B1.

↗ In A2 type =A1+1 (add 1 to the number in A1) then press Enter.

2 should appear in cell A2.

↗ Highlight cells A2 down to A12 and click on **Edit** then **Fill** then **Down**.

The numbers 2 to 12 appear in these cells, because each cell is now the cell above + 1.

↗ Highlight cells B1 down to B12 and click on **Edit** then **Fill** then **Down**.

The 19 times table appears in these cells. You can now see that 12 x 19 is 228.

2 Now find the sum of all the numbers in column B:

B1 + B2 +... + B12.

Summing numbers

There are three ways of doing this. You can:

↗ click on B13 followed by the AutoSum button Σ

↗ **or** click on B13 and type in the formula =SUM(B1:B12)

↗ **or** type = in cell B13 and then select **SUM** from the function menu to the left of the formula bar. (Look at all the other functions while you are there.)

3 Use the Help menu to find out what these four functions do and when you might use them.

LOOKUP	SUMIF
IS	TRUE

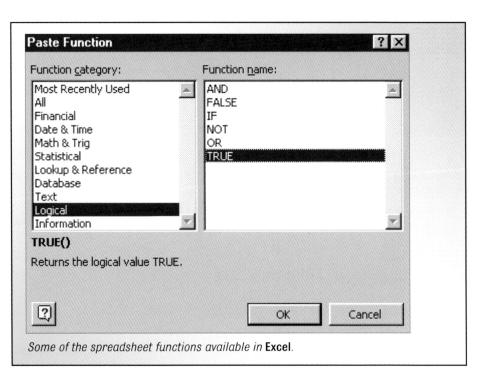

Some of the spreadsheet functions available in **Excel**.

Absolute and relative reference

	A	B	C	D
1	**Percentage**	0.043		
2				
3	**Grade**	**Current hourly pay**	**Pay rise**	**New pay**
4	A	3.2	=B4*B1	=B4+C4
5	B	3.8	=B5*B1	=B5+C5
6	C	4.2	=B6*B1	=B6+C6
7	D	4.3	=B7*B1	=B7+C7
8	E	5.3	=B8*B1	=B8+C8

When you use a cell name in a formula, for example =A3*6, the cell name you use is called the cell reference.

When you created the 19 times table you entered A1*19 in cell B1. You then highlighted the B column and used **Edit** then **Fill** then **Down**. This told the computer to change the cell reference A1 to A2 to calculate A2*19 for cell B2, then to A3 to calculate the value for B3, etc. This cell reference is called a relative reference. The value multiplied by 19 in each B cell is the value in the A cell next to it.

Sometimes you may want to create a formula where a value does not change but is always taken from the same cell. This is known as an **absolute reference**. To keep this value the same, type the $ sign either side of the column letter. For example A1 keeps the reference A1.

Viewing formulae

↗ To see the formulae used in a spreadsheet, click on **Tools** then **Options** then **View** then **Formulas**.

Suppose an employer wishes to give all workers on every grade a 4.3% rise in pay. This spreadsheet makes the calculation easy:

	A	B	C	D
1	Percentage	4%		
2				
3	Grade	Current hourly pay	Pay rise	New pay
4	A	£ 3.20	£ 0.14	£ 3.34
5	B	£ 3.80	£ 0.16	£ 3.96
6	C	£ 4.20	£ 0.18	£ 4.38
7	D	£ 4.30	£ 0.18	£ 4.48
8	E	£ 5.30	£ 0.23	£ 5.53

You can see here see that although the first cell reference in the formula in the 'Pay rise' column changes from B4 to B5 to B6, etc, this value is always multiplied by the amount in cell B1 because it was entered as B1 in C4.

Skills practice

1 Enter the data from the pay rise example above into a spreadsheet.

Conduct a 'What If analysis' by altering the pay increase by 1% at a time from 5% to 20%.

Your IF statement should display 'Acceptable increase' if the overall rise in annual pay for the lowest paid grade does not exceed £1000. 'Unacceptable increase' should show if the rise exceeds £1000.

Note: to calculate annual pay, you need to know that each person works 37 hours per week for 48 weeks of the year.

2 Design a spreadsheet to show your personal school timetable. Try to use all the techniques demonstrated so far. Print out a copy for your folder.

3 Create your school timetable as a table in *Word*. Once you have created your timetable in both packages, compare:

- how easy it was to create
- the final result
- how easy it is to resize
- how easy it is to change.

4 Collect information on all the students in your ICT group. Create a spreadsheet that displays the information in columns with these headings:

a First name

b Family name

c Gender (male/female)

d Hair colour

e Eye colour

f Favourite school subject (other than ICT)

Colour the cells for hair and eye colour.

Now use the sort function to:

- Put the students into alphabetical order by family name.
- List the girls before the boys.
- Find how many girls have black hair.
- Find the favourite school subjects for any blue-eyed boys in your group.

Charts and graphs

You can use a spreadsheet to create charts and graphs.

- Bar charts show numbers of items.
- Line graphs show trends over time.
- Pie charts show percentages or fractions of a whole.

Local Authority income and expenditure

Here are some facts and figures about a typical local authority's income and spending.

Out of every £ spent: 61p was on education; 14p on Social Services; 9p on highways and transport; 5p on police; 3p on fire; 2p on libraries and 6p on other services.

Out of every £ of income: 33p came from Council tax; 22p from property taxes; 25p from Central Government grants and 20p for charges for services.

These are much easier to analyse if you present them in a chart.

A pie chart is used because it shows the relative size of each component of expenditure compared to the whole.

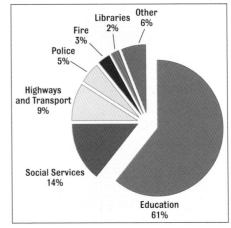

Creating a pie chart

↗ Enter the data into a standard spreadsheet.

↗ Highlight the headings and the data for each item.

↗ Click on the Chart button, the Chart Wizard button, or click on **Insert** then **Chart**.

↗ Select Pie and the type of pie chart required.

For a pie chart you do not need a key (*Excel* calls this the 'legend'). The segments are labelled with %. You can move the labels around if you need to by clicking and dragging each one in turn.

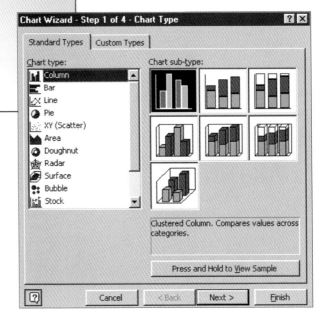

Spreadsheet calculations

1 Collect the names and dates of birth of all the students in your ICT group. Make sure the date of birth is in the format day/month/year, e.g. 19/04/88.

Write the names and dates on pieces of paper and lay them out on a table with each student's date of birth next to his or her name.

- Arrange the names in alphabetical order. Keep the birth dates with the names.
- Convert the dates of birth to this format: 19-Apr-88
- In a third column list the number of years old for each student.
- In a fourth column fill in the number of complete months since their last birthday.
- In a fifth column use an appropriate formula to calculate the age of each student in complete months.
- Now use a formula to calculate the average age of students in your class.

2 How easy were these tasks without a spreadsheet?

3 Try these tasks again using a computer. How much quicker was it?

The London Eye.

London Eye trip

A teacher is planning a class trip to the London Eye during half term. How much will each student have to pay?

- The students will go in a 55-seater coach, which will cost the same to hire whether or not it is full.
- The entrance fees will be £4.50 for each student.
- Each student will need insurance, at 15p per student.

- The entry fee of £9.50 for each adult will also be paid by the students. There will have to be at least one adult of each gender and at least one adult for every 12 students on the trip.
- Lunch will cost £4.50 each for students. Adults will buy their own.

SCHOOL TRIP CALCULATOR

Trip		British Airways London Eye	
Number of students [Maximum 50]	50	Student to adult ratio [min 2]	12
Number of adults	5	Insurance premium [per student]	£0.15
		Lunch	£4.50
	£		£
Student entrance fee	£4.50	Total student fees	£225.00
Adult entrance fee	£9.50	Total adult fees	£47.50
Cost of coach			£354.00
Cost for student			£17.18

With this model you can carry out 'What If analysis'. By putting sample figures or test data into the model you can see what will happen to the cost per student if different factors change.

Construct this spreadsheet model. Use it to find out the cost per student in these situations:

1 The number of students drops to 43.

2 The cost of the coach increases to £415 due to fuel price increases.

3 You go during low season and the entrance fee for each adult is reduced to £8.50 (student fees remain unchanged).

4 Students decide to bring their own lunch.

5 The minimum student to staff ratio is 1:15 not 1:12.

16 Processing and presenting data

In this unit you will:
- discover what a database is
- learn how to create a database
- use standard database features such as fields, entities, and records.

11 **Data** is any recorded facts and figures about people, objects and events. One of the most widely used databases is the telephone directory. What makes this a very useful database is the way it is organised. You can quickly find a person's telephone number if you know their family name, because the entries in the directory are in alphabetical order.

Your details are currently on several databases in school. You are on a class list or register that your teacher keeps. You are also on the school's central computer database. The school uses this to find contact numbers for parents and doctors in emergencies. It also allows them to keep a check on the total number of students and to calculate school income (which depends on the number of students).

Storing data

The computer software that enables you to record and manipulate data effectively is known as a data-handling program or database application. The database is the data held within the program.

We use computers to collect and store data because they can:

- store large amounts of data
- find and display data quickly
- be updated easily
- search for data by different criteria
- present data in a variety of ways.

Computers can also be linked so that everyone in an office can access the database, and many people can use the data at the same time. Using the Internet the database can be accessed anywhere in the world.

One of the largest databases in the UK is the *Shoppers Survey*, which has millions of records about people's shopping habits. The information is collected through postal questionnaires and stored on a large mainframe computer. A mainframe computer is used for processing large quantities of data, but is not suitable for general interactive uses.

Office databases allow many users to input and access data at the same time.

Databases

A database is a collection of information. Each person or object included in the database is called an entity. The information stored for each entity on is called a record. The record is usually divided into several different pieces of data, called fields.

Creating a database

First you must collect the data. An effective way of doing this is by **questionnaire**. It is important that you plan your questionnaire carefully so that it will collect all the data you need for your database.

Before you start to create the database, plan the fields that you will use for the information. Which type of data will go in each field? One field may need to contain text, another may take a date, numbers, or currency. If you are asking **closed questions** you may only need a yes or no answer in some fields.

In a telephone directory the entities are the people, organisations and businesses that have a telephone. The record kept for each entity contains five fields:

1 Name
2 House/building number
3 Street
4 Town
5 Telephone number(s)

Before you can input the data, you need to tell the database program what sort of data each field will contain. If you set up a number field, for example, you won't be able to enter letters into it. When you enter data into a field, the database program will validate the data. This means it will check to make sure that the data is of the correct type, and refuse the data if it isn't. This is important as your calculations based on a number field would fail if it contained words instead.

Field	Field type
Car make	Text
Car price	Currency
Car colour	Text
Has it a valid MOT?	Yes /No
Has it a current tax disc?	Yes /No

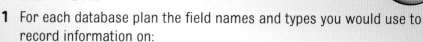

Field work

1 For each database plan the field names and types you would use to record information on:

- a register of students who attend your ICT lessons
- a family telephone address book
- a 'birthday' book
- a school multimedia club.

2 You are creating a database for an under-13 football club. Why would it be better to have the field 'date of birth' rather than 'age'?

Creating your own database

The owner of a car sales firm buys cars from classified advertisements in the local paper and sells them at a higher price on the car lot. He sets up a database to help him find the most suitable car for a customer. He uses *Access®*, the data handling program in Microsoft® *Office*.

His database includes the price he paid for the car, so he can make sure he doesn't sell at a loss.

Mitsubishi Galant GTI 16 valve, 1991, 4 wheel drive, 4 wheel steer, 73,000 miles FSH MOT **£4450**

Land Rover Series 1 1955 LWB pickup Full MOT **£2195**

BMW Compact 316I 1995 alpine white FSH 18,000 miles **£9500**

Renault 19 16v 1993 MOT **£3000**

Ford Montego Estate 1990 2.0 Gsi Racing green **£600**

Ford Sierra 1800L 1989 MOT V.G.C. **£500**

Nissan Sunny 1.4 GS 1990 stereo, electric windows, central locking, 96,000 miles, **£750**

Peugeot 309 GLD Turbo 1993 72,000 miles, midnight blue, MOT, sunroof, electric windows, central locking **£1350**

Renault Laguna RT 1.9 TDI 1998 dark green metallic, 50,000 miles, FSH, electric windows, sunroof, central locking, VGC **£7500**

Citroen BX Turbo Diesel 1989 silver grey MOT electric windows sunroof central locking, **£1200**

Renault 19 16v Chamade 1991 electric sunroof & windows, FSH high mileage **£1350**

Rover 420 SLDi 1998 Ocean blue 28,000 miles sunroof, alloy wheels **£8750**

Vauxhall Cavalier 1987 MOT sunroof **£650**

Ford Escort 1.3L 1990 bodywork needs attention **£400**

Ford Escort 1992 90,000 miles, radio/cassette **£1200**

Fiat Panda 750L 1992 MOT **£850**

Nissan Micra S1.3 1993 white, alloy wheels, sunroof, sports seats, 67,000 miles, MOT **£3250**

Rover 216i coupe 1995 metallic blue FSH, airbags electric windows **£4500**

Ford Escort Turbo Diesel 1.8 LX 1994 113,000 miles, central locking, electric windows **£2950**

Peugeot 306 Alpine 1.4 1993 sunroof, 83,000 miles **£2450**

Citroen ZX Turbo Diesel 1997 electric sunroof, 24,000 miles FSH **£5200**

Toyota Celica GT 1987 automatic sunroof, aircon MOT **£2000**

Ford Fiesta Van 1992 Excellent Condition **£1750**

Vauhall Vectra 2.5 V6 Sri 1997 diamond black FSH 40,000 miles Electric windows and mirrors remote central locking ABS aircon CD Sunroof **£8500**

Identifying suitable fields

Look at the car advertisements and list the different fields you need to create a database table.

Setting up tables containing the fields

In *Access* you need to set up tables containing the fields first.
Once the fields have been set up you can input your data.

Setting up tables

- In *Access* 97 set up a new database file, by clicking on **File** then **New Database** and then selecting **Blank database**.

- Then select the tab **Tables**. Click on the **New** button and then choose **Design view**.

- In *Access* 2000 click on **File**, then **New...**, then **Database**.

- In XP select **Blank database** in the task pane.

- In all of *Access* 97, 2000 and XP you will then be asked to save your database with a file name of your choice. Do this and click on **OK**.

- Then select the option **Tables**. Select **Create a table** in **Design view**.

  You are now ready to design the fields in your table.

- Once you have entered all the fields and field types, close the **Design view** window.

- A message will appear to ask you if you want to save your table – click on **Yes**.

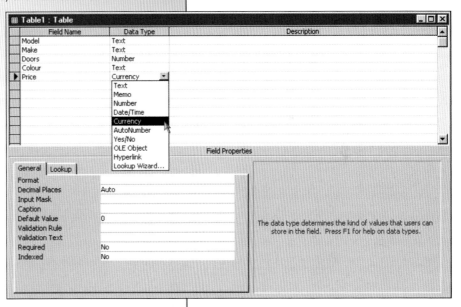

- Enter a name for your table in the dialogue box that appears. Give your table a name which reflects the data you will enter into it: e.g. Car details for a database of cars. Click on **OK**.

- A message will appear warning you that no **primary key** has been defined for this table, and asking if you want to create one. A primary key is a field that is used for indexing and sorting a table. You can click on **No** for now.

- Now you'll see your table, with the name you gave it, listed in the Tables tab.

There are many different data types available for each field. It is important to choose the correct data type.

113

Entering data

Now the fields have been set up you can input your data into the correct fields in your database.

When you enter your data, make sure that the data in each field is entered in the same format each time. For example, in a date of birth field all dates must be entered in the same way. A human would realise that 19th April 1988 is the same as 19-04-88, but the data-handling program might not. If some data is entered in a different format the computer may not be able to analyse it. Once your database is complete, check it thoroughly. This is called verification.

Searching the database

Once you have created a database, you can search through the data to find trends. Businesses look at trends to help them make decisions about the future. If the trend is for people to eat out more, a restaurant business may decide to open a new branch.

You can also search the database to find data that matches a set of criteria. The used car business uses the database in this way, to match customers with cars that suit their needs.

One of the easiest ways to match a set of criteria or look at trends in a database is to use the 'sort' function.

You can sort the cars by price to answer the questions:

- Which is the cheapest car?
- Which is the most expensive car?

Inputting data

↗ Select the **Tables** tab or area.

↗ Select the table you wish to enter data into and choose **Open**. A blank table will appear on screen with the field names at the top of each column.

↗ You can now type your data into this table. Click on a cell and type in the data for that field.

Table1 : Table

	Model	Make	Doors	Colour	Price
	309 GLD	Peugeot	5	Midnight Blue	1350
	Laguna	Renault	5	Dark Green	7500
	Escort	Ford	3	N\a	1200

Sorting

↗ Select the **Tables** tab.

↗ Either double click on the icon for the table holding the car data, or select the table and choose **Open**.

↗ Click on the field containing the cost of the car and the column will turn black. Then click on the Sort Ascending button, A–Z. This will display the cars in price order, lowest price first.

↗ To display the information with highest price first, click on the Sort Descending button, Z–A.

Using simple filters in a database

When you search the data you can use a filter to narrow down your search.

In *Access* you do this using the **Filter By Selection** button, which looks like this:

Instruction box

↗ In your table select one of the criteria you are looking for, e.g. a 3 door car.

Table1 : Table

Model	Make	Doors	Colour	Price
309 GLD	Peugeot	5	Midnight Blue	1350
Laguna	Renault	5	Dark Green	7500
Escort	Ford	3	N\a	1200
*				0

↗ Then *either* click on the **Filter By Selection** button, *or* rightclick and choose **Filter By Selection**.

↗ The table will automatically display all the entries which meet your criteria. Here that is cars with 3 doors:

Table1 : Table

Model	Make	Doors	Colour	Price
Escort	Ford	3	N\a	1200
*				0

↗ Now select your second criterion, e.g. colour red, and do the same again.

By selecting different criteria in turn you narrow down the data until only the cars that are suitable remain.

Once you have this smaller set of records, most data-handling programs have functions for making statistical calculations based on the data. For example, you could calculate the mean (average) price of the used cars for sale.

Library database

Use a data-handling program to create a database of library books.

What fields will you need?

What type of data should each field accept?

Searching data by hand

1 Look at the data on page 112. Can you find a car that fits these criteria?
   - a diesel engine
   - French
   - with a sunroof
   - less than 30 000 miles
   - maximum price £5 500.

   How long did it take you to find the car you needed?

2 What is the difference between verification and validation of data used in a data-handling program?

   How might you notice that data has not been verified?

Designing a questionnaire

One of the most important uses of computers is for storing and analysing data. For the computer to give you accurate information, you first have to input accurate data.

One way of collecting data is to use a questionnaire. A questionnaire is simply a list of questions on a topic. The questions can be printed on a form to fill in, or an interviewer can ask the questions and fill in the answers.

Whichever method you use, you must think carefully about the questions you ask. Designing questions to find out precisely the information you need is an important skill.

When to use a questionnaire

Before you start to design a questionnaire, first ask yourself whether this is the best way of collecting the data you need.

In this unit you will:

- learn how to design a questionnaire to collect data
- learn how to write questions to find out the information you need.

- You want to find out how many people visit a certain shop each day. If you ask the staff they will probably not be able to give an accurate figure, as they will have been too busy working to count their customers. In this case observation would be a better way of collecting the data – sitting outside the shop and noting the number of people entering it.

  Observation is the best method to use if you want precise numbers.

- You want to prepare a report for your headteacher on how life at school could be improved. Interviewing pupils in groups, to see what ideas they come up with, could be the most effective way of collecting data for this.

  Interviewing is the best method to use if you want a wide range of ideas and comments.

You are doing some market research for the school tuck shop. You want to know how often pupils use the tuck shop, how much they usually spend, and the items they buy most often. Getting every pupil to fill in a questionnaire would be a good way of finding this information.

Questionnaires are a good way of collecting information when you are trying to find out facts that require no additional explanation.

Collecting data

For each situation, decide whether a questionnaire, observation or an interview would be the best way of collecting the data.

- Finding out customers' opinions about the taste of a new dessert.
- Logging the number of lorries that pass the entrance to a primary school.
- Collecting information about sporting activities.
- Collecting ideas from students for fund-raising events.
- Collecting ideas from parents for fund-raising events.
- Recording the number of males and females buying clothes from a store, and collecting data about their purchases.
- Finding out whether a person is the best candidate for a job.

Designing a questionnaire

1 First decide what you want to know.

It is important to have a clear picture of what you would like to know before you begin to create your questionnaire. This helps you to write questions that will give you that information.

2 Decide who you will give the questionnaire to.

Your target audience determines how you write the questions. For example, if your questionnaire is only for pupils at your school, asking whether they are married or single is not appropriate.

3 Write the first draft of your questions.

Writing the questions

The leisure and tourism department of the local council want to find out what types of leisure facilities local people would be likely to use. They decide to send a questionnaire to every adult and school-age child in the town.

Here is the first draft of the questions.

It is very difficult to write perfect questions on the first attempt.

Once you have written the first draft you can look at the questions critically and make any changes needed.

Can you see any ways that you would change these draft questions?

1. What is your name?
2. How old are you?
3. What are your hobbies?
4. How often do you play sports?
5. When were you born?
6. How much do you spend on leisure activities each week?
7. Which school do you attend?
8. What are your favourite leisure activities?

Everyone in the leisure and tourism department read the draft questions. Here are some of their comments.

Do we really need to know the person's name? People might give more honest answers if they can be anonymous.

These both ask the same thing. We only need one of these.

We don't need precise ages and people might be embarassed to give their age. Give boxes to tick, e.g. under 10 ☐ 10–17 ☐ 18–30 ☐ 31–50 ☐ over 50 ☐

People could give the same answers to both these. Also they are very open questions and we could get very long answers. For question 3 we could ask them to list up to three hobbies. For question 8 we could give a list of possibilities and ask them to rank them in order of preference.

1 What is your name?

2 How old are you?

3 What are your hobbies?

4 How often do you play sports?

5 When were you born?

6 How much do you spend on leisure activities each week?

7 Which school do you attend?

8 What are your favourite leisure activities?

9 Do you agree that sport is good for you?

This is an open-ended question. People might exaggerate to make themselves sound more healthy. We could give a list of sports and ask them to tick the ones they play at least once a month.

People are not likely to know an exact figure for this. We only need a general idea of what they spend. Give them answers to choose from, e.g. 0–£5 ☐, £6–£10 ☐ £11–15 ☐ £16–£20 ☐ over £20 ☐

This is not relevant. The adults do not attend school.

This question is biased. It encourages people to answer 'yes'.

Things to remember when writing questions

- Avoid asking the same thing twice.
- Avoid sensitive or embarrassing questions.

  Some people might not like giving their age, or their religion, or discussing personal hygiene, for example.

- How easy is it to answer the question? Give boxes to tick, where appropriate.

- For quantities, how accurate do the answers need to be? Give ranges with boxes to tick.

- Should the question be open or closed?

  Closed questions require a simple response, where it is difficult for the respondent to give more than the information you require. Closed questions are often asked at the start of any interview or questionnaire to help the respondent feel comfortable.

  Open questions allow a person to expand on an answer, to give their own opinions or to raise a problem about the question. These types of questions should not be used a lot in a questionnaire as it is difficult to compare people's answers.

- Restrict the range of possible answers by giving a list.

  To find out about people's leisure activities you could use a question like this.

> Which of these leisure activities do you take part in once a month or more? Tick all that apply.
>
> Swimming ☐ Cycling ☐
> Football ☐ Badminton ☐
> Bowling ☐ Cinema ☐
> Theatre ☐ Theme parks ☐
> Other (Please specify) ....

The list acts as a prompt to the person filling in the questionnaire.

You could write a longer list than this, but there would probably still be some activities you had not included. The 'Other' category allows people to give their own activities.

By asking how many activities people take part in once a month or more, you find out which they do regularly, rather than what they may have done once.

- Use ranking to find out about people's preferences.

Another way of finding out about peoples' leisure activities would be with a question like this.

> Rank these activities from 1 to 8. Use 1 for the activity you like the most and 8 for the one you like least.
>
> | | | | |
> |---|---|---|---|
> | Swimming | ❑ | Cycling | ❑ |
> | Football | ❑ | Badminton | ❑ |
> | Bowling | ❑ | Cinema | ❑ |
> | Theatre | ❑ | Theme parks | ❑ |

- Avoid biased questions.

A biased question leads people to give a particular answer, rather than what they really think.

Question 9 could be asked like this instead.
In your opinion, how important is sport for health?
very important ❑ important ❑ not important ❑

Making changes to the draft questions

After taking note of everyone's comments, the questions were changed as shown below.

1 What is your age group?
under 10 ❑ 10–17 ❑ 18–30 ❑ 31–50 ❑ over 50 ❑

2 What are your hobbies? Please list no more than three.

....

3 Which of these leisure activities do you take part in once a month or more? Tick all that apply.

Swimming	❑	Cycling	❑
Football	❑	Badminton	❑
Bowling	❑	Cinema	❑
Theatre	❑	Theme parks	❑

Other (Please specify) ....

4 How much do you spend on leisure activities each week?
0–£5 ❑ £6–£10 ❑ £11–£15 ❑ £16–£20 ❑ over £20 ❑

5 Rank these activities from 1 to 8. Use 1 for the activity you like the most and 8 for the one you like theleast.

Swimming	❑	Cycling	❑
Football	❑	Badminton	❑
Bowling	❑	Cinema	❑
Theatre	❑	Theme parks	❑

6 In your opinion, how important is sport for health?
very important ❑ important ❑ not important ❑

The final version

Once you are happy with the questions you must think about the appearance of the questionnaire.

The layout of a questionnaire is very important. If the reader cannot easily see the next question to answer, or where to answer, they may not bother.

- Questionnaires should be produced in a word processing package, with no typing or spelling errors.

- There should be a short introduction explaining who the questionnaire is for and why they want the information. Use a different typeface for this so it stands out from the questions on the sheet.

- The questionnaire should be as short as possible, so you don't waste people's time.

- The order of questions is important. Start with closed questions that are easy to answer. Next ask any more complex questions and finally more personal questions. This way people are more likely to complete your questionnaire.

- Provide enough space for the answers. If you have boxes to tick or fill in, try to keep them all on the right hand side of the page. This will help you when you begin to collate the answers.

- Add a note at the bottom of the questionnaire to say thank you. The people filling in your questionnaire have given up their own time. Always be polite. You never know when you will need to ask them again.

Finally, step back and take a look at your questionnaire. If possible give it to a friend to try out the questions. What do you think? Does anything distract you? Are the instructions clear?

If it looks bad, or it doesn't work – change it.

Anytown Council
Department of Leisure and Tourism
Survey to discover the demand for
leisure facilities in the town.

Please answer all the questions as accurately as possible. If you are
unable to answer a question, please leave it and go on to the next.

1 What is your age group?

under 10 ❏   10–17 ❏   18–30 ❏   31–50 ❏   over 50 ❏

2 How much do you spend on leisure activities each week?

0–£5 ❏   £6–£10 ❏   £11–£15 ❏   £16–£20 ❏   over £20 ❏

3 In your opinion, how important is sport for health?

very important ❏   important ❏   not important ❏

4 Which of these leisure activities do you take part in once a month or
more? Tick all that apply

Swimming   ❏
Cycling   ❏
Football   ❏
Badminton   ❏
Bowling   ❏
Cinema   ❏
Theatre   ❏
Theme parks   ❏
Other (Please specify) ....

5 Rank these activities from 1 to 8. Use 1 for the activity you like the
most and 8 for the one you like the least.

Swimming   ❏
Cycling   ❏
Football   ❏
Badminton   ❏
Bowling   ❏
Cinema   ❏
Theatre   ❏
Theme parks   ❏

6 What are your hobbies? Please list no more than three.

....

....

Thank you for your time.

Designing questions

1 Re-word these questions so that they can be answered as accurately as possible.

   a How old is your eldest child ?

   b How much frozen food do you buy from the supermarket?

   c How many miles do you walk every week?

   d How many different sports have you played in the last year?

   e Do you wash as well as cook at home?

   f In which age category are you?

   Teenager ❏
   Middle aged ❏
   Pensioner ❏

2 Explain what we mean by a 'closed question'.

3 Why do you think closed questions make people feel more comfortable at the start of a questionnaire?

4 Write four closed questions of your own.

Fast food

You have opened a new fast food resturant in the centre of town.

You want to find out people's opinions on

- your advertising posters
- your plans to have a pavement barbeque every Wednesday when the local market is on.

1 Design the advertising poster for your restaurant.

2 Design a questionnaire to find people's opinions. Test your questionnaire on a friend and make any changes necessary.

3 Get 30 questionnaires completed.

4 Use a spreadsheet or database to graph your data.

5 How do people feel about your plans?
   Are there any surprising results?

6 How easy was it to design your questionnaire?
   Which question was the most difficult to write correctly? Why?

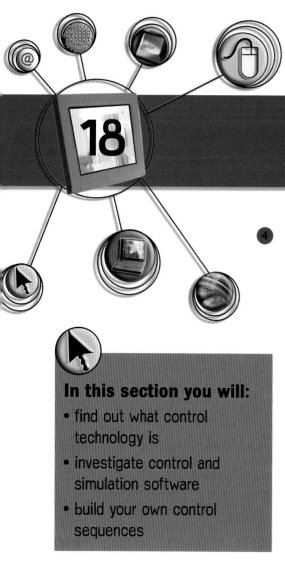

Using control systems

Computers help to **control** more things in everyday life than you may realise. Traffic light systems, aircraft flight, ship navigation, smart card entry to buildings and the London Underground are all controlled by computers to some degree.

A traffic control room. Television screens show the traffic in various parts of the city.

In this section you will:

- find out what control technology is
- investigate control and simulation software
- build your own control sequences

Computers in control

Computers at the heart of control technology do not usually give many signs that they are there at all. These are dedicated or embedded systems that are programmed to do particular jobs.

Types of control system

There are two main types of control system – open loop systems and closed loop systems.

The systems approach

All control systems:

- require information to know what to do   INPUTS
- process given information   PROCESSING
- send out signals to make things work.   OUTPUTS

This systems approach is usually shown as a flowchart:

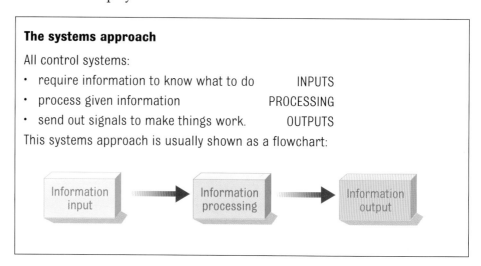

Information input → Information processing → Information output

---

Open loop systems

This is the most simple form of control system. It needs an input to begin a sequence, which is pre-set. The system then processes this information to the output, which is also pre-set.

A personal CD player has an open loop control system.

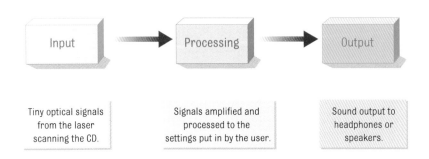

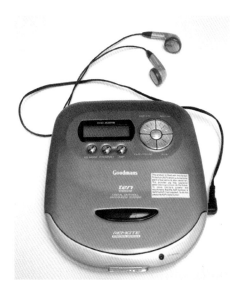

In this system the user sets the volume, tone, etc. The system does not automatically change to compensate for loud or quiet tracks, or switch in and out of mega-bass, or any other preference that you may have. You have to become part of the system and put in your own inputs to get the output that you want.

If you play CDs on a PC you can pre-set your preferences for each CD in your collection into memory. But this technology has not moved into portable equipment … yet.

Closed loop systems

This system monitors itself, using feedback loops, and adjusts its processes accordingly to give the pre-set output.

A modern washing machine has closed loop systems.

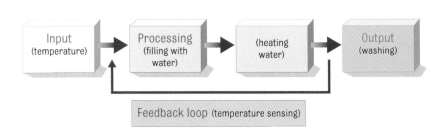

The thermostat monitors the water temperature to ensure it is at the correct level. If not, the system automatically takes action to correct the temperature, either taking in more water from the house supply, or switching on the washing machine's heating system. The washing cycle does not start until the temperature is correct.

Examples of control systems

Control systems in cars

Nearly all cars manufactured since the 1990s have computer-controlled functions. Early control systems in cars included braking systems that helped to avoid skidding. These were known as ABS (Advanced Braking System), or an anti-lock braking system.

Later, engine management systems were developed. These helped to reduce fuel consumption, making cars more economical to run and less polluting.

Nowadays some cars have automatic 'rain-detecting' windscreen wipers and darkness-detecting lights. They can even recognise individual drivers as they get in the car and automatically adjust the seat positions to suit them.

This car's control systems includes ABS, engine management to the make car more economical to run, rain detecting windscreen wipers and darkness detecting lights, plus automatic seat adjustment for individuals.

Fly by wire aircraft technology

Three critical sets of information are needed to fly an aeroplane:

1 The thrust – the force produced by the engines.

2 The lift – produced by the shape of the wings.

3 The flight plan – aircraft weight, destination, route and weather conditions.

These sets of information contain a lot of detail, which can change as the flight progresses. The on-board computers process this information accurately and quickly and the pilot makes any necessary adjustments.

A fly by wire aircraft control system uses electronic systems to translate the pilot's instructions into movements of the control surfaces (e.g. flaps, ailerons, rudder to alter direction and lift) and adjustments to thrust from the engines.

Other aircraft operation systems, such as landing gear, are also controlled electronically. There are no *physical* links from the cockpit to the control surfaces, only devices sending out electronic signals to the appropriate output device.

Some specialist aircraft such as fighters are aerodynamically unstable, which means that they require constant adjustments to the controls to keep them stable during flight. It would be impossible for the flight crew to carry this out, so the aircraft depends upon computers for this task. The onboard computers monitor all the critical functions 1000s of times every second to ensure that the pilot cannot exceed the capabilities of the aircraft. This reduces the stress levels for the pilot and improves performance and safety.

In any aircraft, although the on-board computer makes the pilot's job easier, these systems cannot cope with the unexpected. Therefore the pilot's experience and decision-making skills are vital for safe flight.

Control systems in cameras

Until recently, if you wanted a camera that you could just 'point and shoot', you had to make do with a simple one, that only took good pictures in a very narrow range of photographic conditions. The alternative was to learn about the fundamentals of photography so that you could adjust all the settings yourself.

Modern automatic cameras contain a small computer that measures all the information and sets the controls of the camera to suit.

On board systems help pilots to control sophisticated aircraft.

Camera settings

An automatic camera measures and adjusts for:
- Light conditions
- How far away the subject of the picture is
- The type of film being used
- The background colours and light
- Whether the object is moving or not.

Aircraft control

1 List the data an aircraft flight computer needs for a safe flight.
2 Draw a flowchart showing the open loop system of aircraft control.
3 Draw a flowchart showing the closed loop system that helps fighter aircraft to fly safely.
4 Why do you think that the pilot retains control at the most critical stage of the flight, i.e. take off?
5 What are the advantages of using advanced control systems to fly aircraft rather than requiring the pilot to make all the decisions?

Simulation – testing new control systems

Control systems must be tested before they are put into full operation. Simulation software can model real-life situations in 'virtual reality'. In virtual reality designers can experiment with modifying a system or product until it is to the required standard or specification.

Before simulation software was developed, products were tested by building prototypes and seeing how they worked. This had obvious drawbacks. If the product was not to standard it would have to be redesigned and then another prototype built and tested. This process took time and could be very expensive, particularly for products such as cars and aeroplanes.

A simulation can be repeated many times, with small changes to the simulated variables each time. The results of these changes are recorded and give designers an insight into how a product will perform in different operating conditions and any problems this might cause. The simulation allows them to test safely whether a failure could create a dangerous situation.

Simulation software is also used for practising skills. Aircraft pilots use flight simulators to practise safe flying in difficult and dangerous situations that they may never have experienced in real life. You may have tried a flight simulator at a theme park. Many arcade games use simulators, e.g. for skiing, boat or car racing games.

Simulation is used for entertainment as well as testing and training.

Using control software

Crocodile Clips® software provides simple simulation of electronics and mechanics. It allows you to create designs on screen and then see them behave like the real thing – motors and gears turn, bulbs glow and springs stretch. You can turn up the power to see gears turn faster and bulbs glow brighter but, as in real life, too much power and your components will explode.

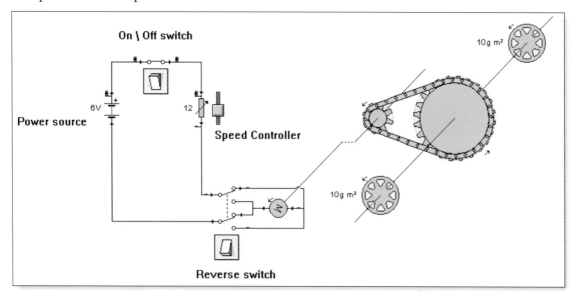

Using *Crocodile Clips* you can:

- Look at the toolbar to see what components are available.

- Choose components for your system by dragging them from the toolbar and link them using your mouse.

- Operate switches and sliders with a touch of the mouse.

- Use animation to see the movement of motors, gears and wheels and the effect on other components in your system, such as lamps. The virtual input devices, e.g. switches and sensors, work like real ones. Once your circuit is completed with the correct inputs your virtual system comes to life on screen. Motors run, lights illuminate, components fail in flames if they are overloaded!

- Select component groups by lassoing them, using the lasso button. With this technique you can copy circuits and import them into a word processor or graphics package to use in reports or diagrams.

Simulation software like this gives you access to a virtual laboratory with the benefits of no loose connections and no faulty components.

Peripheral Interface Controllers

A Peripheral Interface Controller (PIC) system uses microchips that have been pre-programmed to control events.

Using PIC software, you can create an on-screen control flowchart to build, test and edit your own control system. The control sequence you create is translated into a code that can be downloaded into the PIC microcontroller chip via a programmer. The chips are completely self-contained so they can be used to control objects that can move around freely, such as a buggy. They are also reprogrammable so they can be re-used for different projects.

With a PIC sysem you can program microchips to use in your systems.

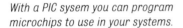

The inputs to the system can come from sensors. You can also build time delays into the control system, so the machine counts a certain time until moving on to the next part of the program. The time countdown can be displayed on an LCD panel if you wish.

The output devices, such as motors, lamps, etc. are connected to the pins of the microchip. Some can be linked directly to the microprocessor; but others have to go through a secondary interface, especially if the device requires a lot of electrical current.

Simple circuits

Use *Crocodile Clips* software to build two simple circuits.

Test your circuits by changing the variables until your circuits stop working.

List the advantages of being able to design and test electro-mechanical systems in this way.

Designing a control system

Effective control systems need to be well planned before the simulation or chip programming stage. Flowcharts are the most effective way of planning a system.

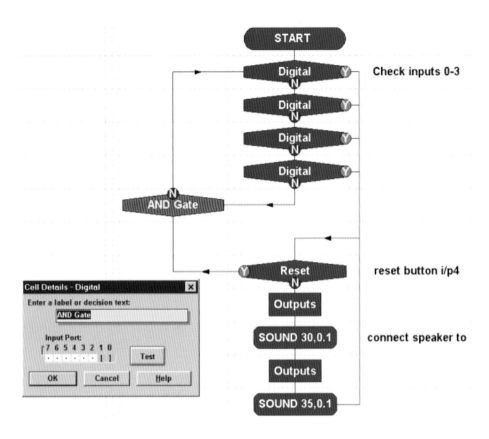

Check inputs 0-3

reset button i/p4

connect speaker to

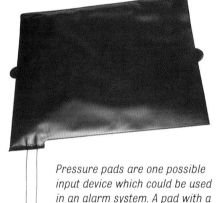

Pressure pads are one possible input device which could be used in an alarm system. A pad with a weight upon it, human or object, causes the control system to respond in a preset way.

An intruder alarm

The pressure pads are set so that they work as a gate. There are two types of gates – 'and gates' and 'or gates'.

- **and gate**: more than one sensor must be triggered to energise the system.

- **or gate**: only one of a set of sensors has to be triggered to energise the system.

The pressure pads work as an 'or gate'. If an intruder steps on any one of them the circuit is energised and the alarm will sound.

Resetting the system uses an 'and gate'. Two input switches have to be pressed at the same time for the reset command to operate.

PIC system commands

You will need to use some of the following commands to build a control sequence.

Start

The flowchart starts at the START command. Every flowchart must have a START command.

End

The flowchart will stop running whenever an END command is reached. An end box indicates that this is where the system terminates. The alarm system does not have an end box because the system is expected to run permanently. However, you could insert another decision box to indicate if the alarm was switched off and stop the circuit operating.

Wait

A wait command makes a running flowchart pause for the time specified before carrying out the next command. You can use it to keep output devices switched on or off for a set time.

Reset

In a circuit such as the alarm system, once the alarm has been triggered you need to reset the system. The criteria for this decision box are: If the system is reset (possibly by a button or switch), then go back to checking the sensors for intruders. If the system is not reset, then the decision box allows the output (the sound) to be triggered.

Decision boxes

These commands test the state of a sensor connected to an input pin on a PIC microcontroller. They are vital in closed loop control systems.

Decision boxes choose between two alternatives. This digital decision box is used with a digital sensor. When data reaches this point, the decision box allows the circuit to be continued in only one of two directions, Y or N. The data is tested to make the decision on which way to go.

For example the testing criteria may be 'if the sensor is activated continue on the Y route'. The green coloured number 1s show that in this case the sensor is active and pins 7 and 5 show a 1 to indicate this.

Output

An output command switches the output devices connected to the PIC microcontroller on or off. Many components can be used as output devices, for example buzzers and motors. In the alarm system a speaker is used to output sound.

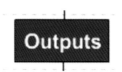

Sound

This element is set up with instructions about how long the sound should last and at what volume and frequency. Two boxes are used to vary the sound and make it warble.

Motors

The motor command allows you to use two output pins on a PIC microcontroller to switch a motor to forwards, reverse or off.

Putting it all together

For your system to work effectively you need to indicate the route for your flowchart to operate. Do this by drawing arrows between the commands. Look at the alarm system flowchart on page 131 to see the arrows indicating the way the system should operate.

Controlling objects

Produce control sequences for:

1 traffic light sequences

2 a cooling fan for a conservatory

3 a burglar alarm with sensors.

Remember to plan each system before you start to create the program sequences on screen. Think carefully about how you use feedback loops.

Computers in control

Task 1

Make a list of 10 systems you think use computer control.

From your list select two and investigate what exactly is controlled.

For example:
A car probably has three categories of control system:

1 Efficiency and reliability systems: security, engine, gearbox, fuel, etc.

2 Safety: brakes, airbags, de-icers, etc.

3 Comfort: climate control, seat positions, etc.

For the two systems you investigate:

Why have these systems been developed?

What are the advantages?

What are the disadvantages?

Task 2

1 What is a 'point and shoot' camera?

2 How are these cameras different to less sophisticated ones? Why are they popular?

3 Produce an advertisement describing the advantages of an 'idiot proof' camera.

4 Draw a diagram of a point and shoot camera to show:

  • information input

  • process

  • output

19 Creating a presentation

A presentation program lets you produce high quality presentations combining pictures, graphs and charts, text, video, sound and animation. The program has presentation 'templates' you can use, and a library of special effects and sounds.

There are many different types of presentation package. The package most commonly used in schools is *Powerpoint*, which is provided in Microsoft *Office* packages.

In this unit you will:

- learn how to create high quality computer-assisted presentations

Presentations

You can use presentations to report back from a field trip, present findings from some primary research, or for a tutor group assembly. At most business and political conferences you will see a large screen behind the speaker displaying the important points she or he is making, or charts and graphs. Sometimes they are used to project scene titles at the side of the stage during a theatre performance.

You can use a presentation program to:

- produce overhead projector (OHP) slides

- run a slide show on a PC monitor or network

- project a slide show from a PC on to a screen

- run a slide show from a web page link.

A presentation package being used in a business meeting.

Planning a presentation

When planning your presentation you must always keep in mind how the audience will see it. Keep text large enough to read, diagrams simple and pictures clear. Any animation you use should amuse and attract attention, and sounds should compliment the slide.

You should always plan your presentation before you begin to create it, to get an idea of how it will look. Do this by storyboarding – draw each of your slides as you would like them to look on screen, and make notes on the drawings to indicate the size of text and types of animation you would like to use.

Using *Powerpoint*

Starting a new presentation

- ↗ Load the program and click on **File** then **New**.
- ↗ In *Powerpoint* 97 and 2000 select **General** then **Blank Presentation**.
- ↗ In *Powerpoint* XP a Task pane opens up on the right of the window. Click on **New** and **Blank Presentation** there.

For *Powerpoint* 97:
- ↗ Select **blank presentation** in the options box which appears on screen.
- ↗ Then select **OK**.
- ↗ Choose a blank layout.

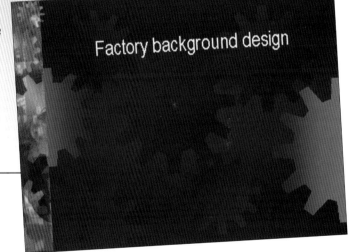

Factory background design

You can choose a different design for each slide, but this may confuse your audience. It is often best to use one design throughout the presentation.

Setting a slide style

- ↗ Choose the type of slide you want – text, bullet points, picture, etc.
- ↗ Click on **Format** and then **Apply Design** (in *Powerpoint* 97) or **Apply Design Template** (in *Powerpoint* 2000) or **Style Design** (in *Powerpoint* XP). Choose any design or style.

The presentation shown above uses a notebook design. There are 17 designs to choose from and when you have had practice you can create your own.

Adding text

Some of the tool bars in *PowerPoint* are the same as in *Word*. If you have chosen a style template that contains text boxes it will tell you to click and add text. If you want to add additional text or if you start with a blank template, simply add a text box by selecting **Insert** then **Te_x_t box.** Or a *WordArt* box by selecting **Insert** then **Picture** and then **WordArt**.

Once you have an active text box, you can alter the text font and colour.

Remember the slides must be easy to read, often from a distance.

Follow these simple rules:
1 Keep the font size large (22+).
2 Keep text to a minimum – use bullets to make main points.
3 Choose a simple font that is clear and easy to read.
4 Choose a font colour that compliments and stands out from the design background colour.

Because the program is based on *Word* it will highlight spelling mistakes and grammatical errors in the normal way, so make sure you correct these.

Planning presentations

1 When you choose the slide design, you need to consider the type of presentation you are giving. For example, if your presentation is on dolphins you can have the sea as a background.

Design or describe background designs for these topics:
 • students being welcomed to a new school
 • litter
 • the opening of a new school theatre
 • the launch of a record or CD
 • a geography field trip
 • a foreign exchange trip
 • astronomy
 • a sporting event.

2 Think of a theme for a class assembly and plan the 12 slides you will show. Describe in detail the backgrounds you will use, as well as the fonts and font sizes.

Suitable themes are:
 • caring for the environment
 • dealing with bullying
 • New Year, Easter, Diwali, Christmas, Eid or other celebrations
 • topical news issues.

Adding pictures

Pictures illustrate your presentation and help to keep the audience's attention. *Powerpoint* can use the pictures in different ways, such as making the picture appear unexpectedly, accompanied by an amusing sound.

Inserting pictures

↗ Click on **Insert** and then **Picture**.

↗ Select **ClipArt** or select your own files using the option **From file** and browsing to find the file you want.

Adding animation

Animation makes slide shows more interesting – whether on the PC screen or projected on to a wall screen.

Once you have created a slide you can decide how the various parts – text, pictures, charts, etc – can build on screen in front of the audience.

Follow these stages:

Inserting pictures.

Animation

For *Powerpoint* 97 or 2000

↗ Choose the **Slideshow** menu and then **Custom Animation**.

↗ For *Powerpoint* 97 click on **Timing**. In the box you will see all the components of your slide. Click on the components one at a time and then select **Animate**.

↗ For *Powerpoint* 2000 the components of your slide are listed in the dialogue box. You need to click in the boxes next to any that you want to animate, so that the box is checked (ticked).

↗ Use the Timing tab (*Powerpoint* 97) or Orders and Timing tab (*Powerpoint* 2000) to specify whether the animation should happen automatically after a certain time, or when you click the mouse.

↗ The slide components will now appear in the Animation order box (*Powerpoint* 97 and 2000). To change the order, click on the component and then change the order by clicking on the arrows.

↗ Once the animation order is correct, click on the first component and then **Effects**.

Animation.

Animation

For Powerpoint XP

↗ Choose the **Slideshow** menu and then **Custom Animation**.

↗ Select the item you wish to animate and choose an animation effect, or select **More animation** for further animation choices.

↗ The slide components are listed in the task pane, and you can use the **Reorder** buttons underneath the list to reorder them.

↗ Once this is done you can use the arrow that appears to edit the timing or effects used in the animated effect chosen.

↗ To do this:

  • Select the down arrow at the side of the animation you have chosen
  • Select Effect options from the drop down menu.
  • A window will appear with option tabs: Effect, Timing and Text animation (if you are animating text).
  • Choose one of these tabs and make changes to the settings for this animation type.

↗ You can also change the sound effects available when that piece of animation is running.

↗ For text you can make the words appear a letter or a word at a time, or all at once. You will find options for this under the Introduce text tab.

Now you can choose your sounds and effects – have fun!

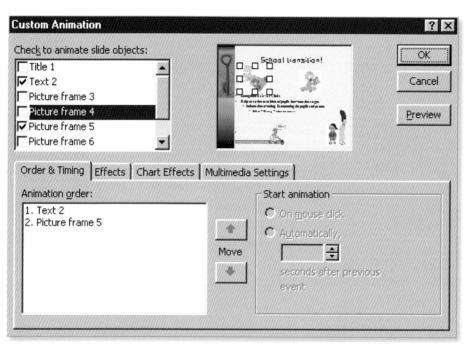

Choose the items to animate by selecting the objects in the Order & Timing tab.

Adding new slides

Once you have created and animated one slide, continue your presentation on additional slides. Do this by clicking on Insert then New Slide. When you do this your old slide is hidden and a new page appears. Select the artwork slide sort button to view thumbnails – small images of all the slides you have created. ▦

Charts

You may want to use charts in your presentation. In *Powerpoint* 97 or 2000, insert your chart and then select the Chart Effects tab to animate it. This allows the elements of the chart to be introduced one at a time – in series. For example, each column of a bar chart can 'wipe up', or grow upwards one at a time.

In *Powerpoint* XP select the Chart Animation tab in the Effect options area.

Once each slide is animated you need to choose how to move from slide to slide. This is known as 'slide transition'. Choose the Slide Show menu and select Slide transition. A screen will appear, giving you similar options to the one below.

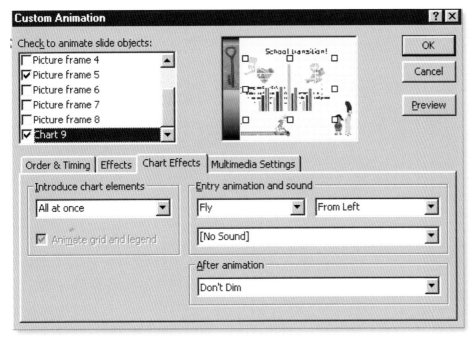

Although they look different Powerpoint 97, 2000 and XP allow almost identical options for slide transition.

Changing the order of play

The slide sort button ⊞ at the bottom left-hand edge of the window loads all of the presentation in tiny format. By clicking and holding the left-hand mouse button you can move the slides into any order of play.

Starting the slide show

You can start the slide show either by clicking the slide show button, or by choosing **View Show** from the **Slide Show** menu.

Other effects to try

● The animation effects button allows you to select an animation effect without using the menu bars. This is only available in *Powerpoint* 97 and 2000, not in XP. It offers you a pre-selected list of effects.

● Sound effects are often found on *ClipArt* discs. They have the filename extension .wav. You can load these on to the C: drive or from a CD.

Choose this button to display a list of pre-set animation effects.

Adding sound

For *Powerpoint* 97 and 2000:

↗ In the **Slide Show/Custom Animation** menu, select the Effects tab and under Sound select Other Sounds and then the appropriate drive. If you are networked ask your teacher which drive to use.

For *Powerpoint* XP:

↗ Use the **Slide Show/Custom Animation** menu to add an animation to a component. Then select that component in the task pane list on the right and click on the little down arrow next to it. Click on Effect Options, and either choose a sound from the list, or select Other… to choose a sound from a CD.

● Video sequences can be loaded from a digital camera or from *ClipArt* CDs. Under **Insert** choose **Movies and Sounds** followed by **Movie from gallery** (for *Powerpoint* 97 and 2000), **Movie from Clip Organizer** (*Powerpoint* XP), or **Movie from File**.

● Try 'Spiral' and 'Swivel' animations – investigate what they do.

● If you have *Powerpoint* 97 or a later version you can design animated web pages by saving your presentation as a web page.

Printing your presentations

Once you have completed your presentation you may wish to print it.

A presentation is often accompanied by a talk, so the slides themselves hold little information. If this is so, you don't have to print each slide in your presentation on a full page. *Powerpoint* allows you to print your whole presentation on as few pages as possible. In order to to this click on **File** and then **Print**.

Select All in the Print range box to print the whole presentation, or use the other selection buttons to print specific parts of it.

To print your slides, in the Print w̲hat box select Handouts. Then in the area labelled Handouts select the number of slides you would like printed on each page. The images to the right of the dropdown option box show how the slides will be laid out on the page.

Once all this is completed, click on OK.

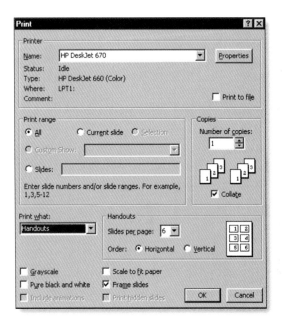

Class assembly

Produce the class assembly you planned on page 136. Remember to use a variety of sources for art and spectacular effects.

If you have access to a digital camera it is always better to take your own pictures to illustrate a point.

Animated children's story

Create a storyboard for an animated children's story presentation.

Using no more than 10 slides, write a story with animated images, text and *WordArt*. Highlight on your storyboard:

• Different text sizes and styles.

• The types of animation you would like to show.

• Different sound effects or music you might use.

Write a short piece about the age group of your audience. Indicate how you have taken them into account when thinking about the words and images you would use.

Finally, indicate what hardware and software you would need to show this presentation to a class.

Navigating on the Internet

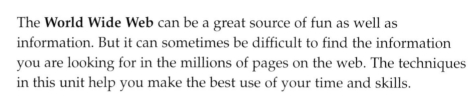

The **World Wide Web** can be a great source of fun as well as information. But it can sometimes be difficult to find the information you are looking for in the millions of pages on the web. The techniques in this unit help you make the best use of your time and skills.

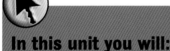

In this unit you will:

- learn to use web addresses and view web pages
- find out about the most important features of a web page, e.g. hyperlinks, URLs
- learn about the tools that make using the web easier
- learn search skills to use on the WWW.

Finding a web page

Each page in each website has a Uniform Resource Locator (URL), which is a web address for that page. Your web browser should have a space at the top of the page where URLs appear when you log on to different pages. It will look something like this.

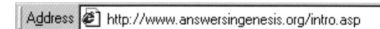

Address http://www.answersingenesis.org/intro.asp

Just like an ordinary address, each part of the URL is important.

- **http://** Most web addresses start with this. It tells the browser that it should expect to read a web document.
- **www** indicates that the page is found on the world wide web and not on your local machine.
- The next part of the URL identifies the website and where it can be found. For example:

HarvySteer.co.uk	A company's website (.co) in the UK (.uk).
John3-16.DreInt.co.uk	A personal website. DreInt is the Internet Service Provider (ISP).

- The final part of the URL is the document on the website you want the browser to read. This is the file name the web designer used to save the documents. Common types are Index.html and Page1.html.

Once you know the URL you can go straight to the page you want. Type the URL into the address bar on your browser and your computer will find and load the page.

Finding your way around the page

Once you have found the web page you can move around it using the hypertext. The hypertext is the words and phrases printed in a different colour so they stand out from the text. When you put the cursor over hypertext it will change shape.

If you click on the hypertext you will move to another part of the web page or website where there is more information on that subject. When hypertext works in this way it is called a hyperlink. A hyperlink is anything that moves you to another place on the page when you select it.

Hyperlinks are a way of organising the page so that readers can move quickly to the parts they want to read, rather than having to read the whole document.

Look at the web page below. It has several hypertext links. Suppose that you are looking for some games to play. The word 'games' is hypertext and links to online games. If you click on it you will move to the online games part of the website.

The hypertext links make web pages easy to use, but if there are a lot on a page it can be confusing. Often they are designed so that they change colour once you have selected them. This makes it easier to see which links you have read and which you still have to follow up.

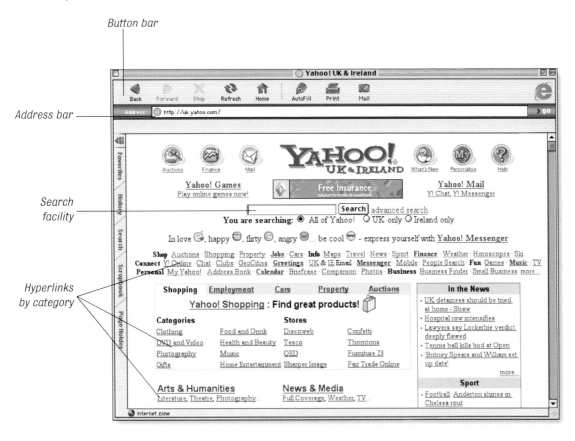

Button bar

Address bar

Search facility

Hyperlinks by category

Favourites, bookmarking or linking

These allow you to mark your favourite web pages, so you can find them quickly another time.

You can create a link which will take you to the page or site marked when you select it. If you select the favourites button on the toolbar, a list of your links will appear. To create a link highlight the URL and drag it on to the link bar, or add a link into a favourites list.

History

Most web browsers have a history section. Here the browser keeps a list of all the web pages visited, with the URL of the website and the date of the visit. This feature is useful if you want to return to a site but have forgotten the URL.

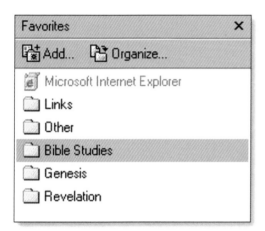

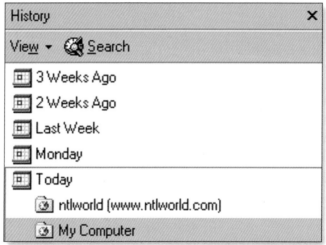

The history function is useful if you forget to bookmark a page.

Favourites

Complete these tasks using *Internet Explorer*.

If you have another web browser, see how many you can complete.

1 Ask your teacher for the URL of an interesting site.

2 Enter the URL in the address bar of your browser.

3 Once the page has loaded, select a hypertext link on the page.

4 Use your mouse to click on the hypertext link and drag it up to a blank space on the links bar.

Now you have made a button on the links toolbar.

5 Now move this link into the favourites folder. To do this, select the favourites button and drag the link into the favourites menu box.

6 Now ask your teacher for another URL and type it in the address bar.

7 Experiment with the Add and Organize buttons in the favourites menu. What do they do?

8 Select the history button. Then select Today.

Count how many Internet sites have been accessed today on your computer.

9 How far back does your history box allow you to look?

The Home button

Whenever you connect to the Internet you start on the home page. This is usually the page for the company providing your Internet access. Clicking on the home button will return you to the home page.

The search button

Selecting this option in your web browser gives you access to some of the most popular search engines. Searching is covered in more detail on pages 146–9.

URLs

1 You have been asked to look at a web page at this destination:

computer:	CJ-Tech.co.uk
web page:	Index.html

What URL would you type in the address box?

2 Look at this URL for a web page.

Address 🔳 http://www.oup.co.uk/secondary/megabyte/index.htm

a Which part of the address identifies this site as being on the web?

b What is the document name?

c What do you think the URL for page 2 is likely to look like?

3 Why is it useful to create links or lists of favourite URLs?

4 a What is the difference between the history feature and the favourites feature of a web browser?

b When would it be most useful to use the history function?

- When you have forgotten the URL for a website you visited recently.
- When you wish to revisit a site you use every day.
- When you want to search the web.
- When you want to return to your ISP's home page.

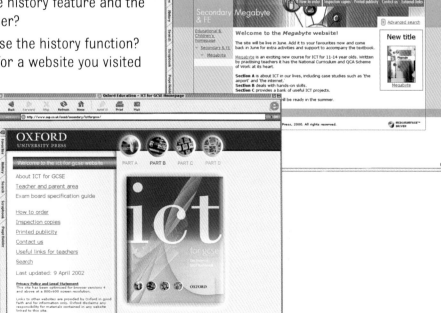

Searching the web

The WWW is an excellent source of information, but it is so large that it is almost impossible to find the page you want without help. A search engine can help you find the information you want.

A search engine is rather like a sales assistant. Suppose you wanted to buy a book on a certain topic. There are hundreds of books on this topic and you are not sure which one would match your specific needs. A good sales assistant will ask you questions about your requirements and narrow your search down to a few books that may be of interest.

A search engine is a huge database of websites. Given a topic, it can suggest websites which may be suitable. However, unlike a good shop assistant, the search engine cannot think for itself or ask you for more information to help narrow down the choice of sites. You need to do this yourself by giving the search engine specific search instructions. You do this either by typing key words in a search box, or by selecting hyperlinks. The next section explains in more detail how to do this.

Once the search engine has a topic or key word it searches its database and attempts to match this word or phrase with details it holds about the sites in its database. It then produces a list of all the websites that may be relevant, with a short description of each site. Some of these may not be what you want at all. You need to use your knowledge of the subject and the information given in the description to decide which sites are worth looking at.

Simple searches and key words

Suppose you are searching for websites for a stamp dealer or a collector of model engines. You could use the simple searches below. However the key words are more specific and will probably get you results more rapidly.

Simple searches	Specific Key Word
1 Stamp	Philately
2 Stamp Dealer	
1 Toy trains	Mansfield Railway Society
2 Model Railway enthusiasts	

Simple searches help you gradually narrow down your search to key words and phrases.

Searches using key words will always generate matches and somewhere in those thousands of matches there is likely to be a useful site. A good key word can narrow your search down very quickly, but poor key words make the task longer and more difficult.

Complex search skills

If a simple search does not narrow down the list of suitable web pages to a manageable amount, you can try more specific searches using:

- wild card searches
- Boolean searches
- quotation marks

● *Wild card searches*

Wild cards are used to widen a search. This may be helpful if your key word searches have not found a relevant site.

The most common wild card for Internet searching is *. For example, entering Man* as a search word may access sites on topics such as:

Manchester	Manifold
Manhood	Manila
Mansfield	Mandolin

Wild card searches can be very useful in the early stages of a search. Use them to investigate specific vocabulary which you can then use in a key word search.

For example, if you are searching for space travel you could use the wild card Space*

This could return Space travel, Spaceship, Space age, Space rocket, Spaceman, Space race, etc. This gives you key words that might be more suitable than Space travel; for example Spaceship. If this key word does not work you can try some of the other options.

Entering Man as a search word may access sites for caveman, sportsman and human.*

Search skills

Two students are searching for information on space flight.
Student A use the words Space travel as key words.
Student B uses the name NASA (the North American Space Agency).

1 Which student will get the most web page suggestions from the search engine?

2 Which search is likely to arrive at a suitable site most quickly?

3 If the search word NASA does not provide a website, how could student B make the search more successful?

4 Give an example of why student A's approach would be the most useful in finding websites.

● *Boolean searches*

When you choose the advanced search option in a search engine, the search engines will probably use a Boolean search. In a Boolean search the search engine has to match sites to a series of instructions or criteria described in OR, AND or NOT statements.

This table shows how the different statements lead you to different websites.

Search	What the search engine looks for
Manchester **NOT** United	Sites about Manchester, but not Manchester United
Manchester **AND** United	Looks for sites with the words Manchester and United
Manchester **AND** United **OR** City	Looks for sites with the words Manchester and United *and also* sites with the words Manchester and City

Different search engines have different rules for using Boolean searches. If you choose an advanced search, the search engine will display some information on how to use it. Make sure you read these instructions before you begin.

● *Quotation marks*

Quotation marks ″ ″ tell the search engine to search for websites where the key words appear *exactly* as they do between the ″ ″ .

If you search for Coventry Cathedral without quote marks, you will get sites for Coventry and sites for cathedrals, as well as specific sites for Coventry Cathedral. Using quote marks narrows down the site options given by the search engine.

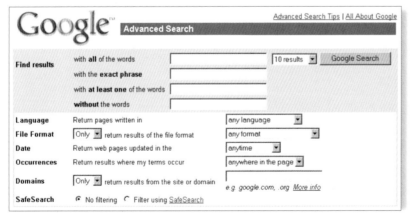

Searching by browsing

Browsing means that you take advantage of information already sorted into categories. Most search engines have hypertext-based browsers, which you can use instead of a key word search. Look for a list of categories in hypertext on the search engine page. For example, selecting Computers could give you a further list of choices such as Software, Peripherals, Components, etc.

Browsing can help you to focus your thoughts. However, its rigid and categorised approach may make it difficult to find the information you require. You may spend some time checking different options related to the topic you are searching for. Searching by browsing is best when you want general information rather than specific details.

The browsing hyperlinks in a popular search engine.

Learning to search

Use the table to plan simple and complex searches for the topics given.

Topic	Key words (Simple search)	Wild card (Complex search)	Boolean (Complex search)	Quotation Marks (Complex search)	Browsing
Scottish Folk Music					
Skiing in New Zealand					
Holiday accommodation in Switzerland					
Free software on the Internet					
How PCs work					

Searching

Use your plan from the 'Learning to search' desk task with an Internet search engine.

For each topic:

*   Which method arrived at suitable search results most quickly?
*   Why do you think there was a difference in the speed and accuracy of the results?

21 The Internet as an information source

Evaluating a website

Once you have found a website, you need to decide whether it is any use to you.

Use this five-point checklist to decide how useful the site is. You can also use it to evaluate any websites you design yourself.

1 Accuracy and content	Are there any spelling errors? Does the information seem correct, based on what you already know? Does the page provide a source to cross check the information against? Is the text used on the site suitable for the intended age and knowledge of the likely audience? Does the site go into enough depth?
2 Originality	Is the website on an unusual topic? Does the website deal with an existing topic differently to other websites? Is there any original research on this site? Is there any information you have not already found elsewhere?
3 Completeness	Is the site still under construction? Does the content of the site change regularly? Do all the hyperlinks work?
4 Navigation	Does the page layout help you to guess where to find information? Does the site have a search engine to help you find the information you want? Does the site have a map, or contents page, showing what the site contains?
5 Instructions	Is there a help page for the site? Is there a Frequently Asked Questions (FAQ) page? Are there details for how to contact the site's author?

Effective web pages

Think about websites you have looked at.

1 How do they convince readers that the site is a reliable and accurate source of information?

2 Explain how these may help a reader to have confidence in a site:

- date last updated.
- qualifications of the author
- bibliography
- a site rating given by a ratings company

Should you believe what you read on a website?

Anyone can make a website and use it to put across their views. It is not always easy to decide whether the information you read on a site is accurate and reliable. Individuals, companies, governments or other groups may use a website to put forward opinions or information that is inaccurate or does not present all sides of an argument. Where information is affected by an opinion, political view or other motive, this information is said to be biased.

Most reliable → **Least reliable**

Traditional references	Governments and Universities	Corporate sites	Individuals' sites
Examples: *Encyclopaedias* *The BBC* *Broadsheet newspapers, e.g. The Guardian* Sites where the operator specialises in collecting accurate and up-to-date information are likely to have the least bias. However, mistakes or personal opinions can sometimes affect the information given.	*Examples:* *Universities* *Government departments* This information is likely to be reliable. It may be biased, as the content may express a political opinion or be a promotional tool. As a check, you should try to obtain further information that supports this from other paper or electronic sources.	*Examples:* *Charities* *Business sites* *Research bodies* This information is likely to be accurate, but may be biased. Beware especially of corporations who are trying to sell something, or of charities who are trying to shock you. They may be selective about the information they display, rather than giving you the whole picture.	These sites are extremely useful. Most sites you view on any given topic will be in this category. However the information they contain may be inaccurate. The authors of the web page may be using it to put forward their own personal views and the information they give may be out of date. Always cross check with information from other, more reliable sources.

How reliable are websites? A rough guide.

Checklist for websites

The guide above will help you determine how reliable the information on a website is. But there is no substitute for common sense. When you are searching for information on a topic, ask yourself these questions:

1. How much do I know about the topic? Do I know enough to confirm that the information on this site is correct?

2. Do I have other information to help me decide how accurate the site is, e.g. library books, newspaper articles?

3. Is this website created by a respected body, e.g. the BBC, a university?

4. Can I spot any evidence of bias or personal opinion in the site?

5. Does this site link to other, more reliable sites, with the same information?

Types of website

Not every website is solely an information source. There are also sites for entertainment, shopping and chatting to others. You may come across some of these:

● *Games play*

Many computer games now allow you to use the Internet to compete against each other.

There are also websites that allow you to take part in games with less complex graphics, such as cards or chess.

● *Online libraries*

Online libraries are reliable information sources. Some have a wide range of information, but others focus on specific topics. They are useful reference sources for checking information found on other websites. Their information is as reliable as an encyclopaedia.

● *Online education*

Many companies or colleges have websites providing online training and education.

● *Online shopping sites*

Shopping on the Internet and e-commerce is big business. Many companies now have sites where you can purchase goods and have them delivered to your home.

● *Online communities*

Web users with common interests often collect their web pages together to form an online community. These are good places to find chat rooms, newsgroups and mailing lists for topics that interest you.

● *Mailing lists*

Signing up to a mailing list on a given topic enables you to discuss that topic online with others. Anything that one member of the list says is sent to all the other members, so that they can reply if they wish. Take care, because a popular list can generate over 50 emails a day!

● *Newsgroups*

These are similar to mailing lists. People use them to discuss topics of interest, but all the comments are stored online instead of being emailed to all the participants. Anyone can post information to a newsgroup, so they can be useful places for finding the answers to your questions.

● *Chat rooms*

Chat rooms are a great place to meet people online, as well as to find out information. There are thousands of chat sites on the Internet. Messages posted to chat rooms can usually be seen by everyone.

When you chat with others online you need to follow some basic rules, known as 'netiquette'. These are explained on page 154.

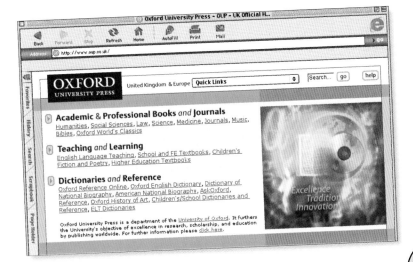

Planning to use websites

1 Web directories are books that list hundreds of useful websites. They are useful when you are planning the sites you could use to research a topic.

Use a web directory to find URLs for sites that would be good sources for these topics:

- animal rights
- showjumping
- Davis Cup tennis

2 Use the diagram for 'Should you believe what you read on a website' on page 151.

For each site you found in question 1, decide what category it is in – Corporate site, University, etc.

3 Why do you think you would obtain more for web page created by individuals results from a search engine than from the a website directory?

4 How easy was it to find suitable references for the topics?

5 Which topic was it most diffcult to find sites for?

Why do you think this was?

6 What were the main advantages and disadvantages of using the website directory to plan the sites you would use for research?

Netiquette

Netiquette is about respect for other people online. It can be easy to offend in emails, because there is no face to face contact, so people cannot see whether you are joking or not. Follow the netiquette rules of the web to ensure that you and others enjoy your time online.

'Etiquette' is a slightly old-fashioned word meaning a code of good manners. 'Netiquette' means the code of manners to use on the Internet.

Most netiquette rules relate to chat rooms, newsgroups and email. They are similar to the rules most people follow in daily life. Swearing in chat rooms is discouraged, and sending unwanted emails or making unwanted advances to others online is the height of bad manners. Also, you shouldn't break the law online (see the section on plagiarism on the next page) and you should pay for any downloads that are not freeware.

Netiquette rules also protect you when you are using the net. Conventions such as observing for a while before you join conversations and ensuring you know where you are on the Internet, mean that you can decide whether an online conversation is one you can safely join. This may sound silly, but the Internet is open to everyone, including people you would not usually choose to speak to. Take care where you chat. Being Web Wise is important for all web users.

WWW Web Wise Netiquette

Remember:

1 Never give out personal information, such as your name, address, email address, telephone number.

2 Do not give out your password or login details.

3 Do not respond to messages which offend you.

4 Act responsibly on the net. Remember other users have feelings too.

5 Never agree to meet people from the Internet.

6 Do not send pictures of yourself over the Internet without a teacher's approval.

Plagiarism and the web

The WWW contains millions of websites with interesting pictures, page designs and other information, and it can be tempting to take these ideas and use them in your own web pages. But you need to observe netiquette and understand the laws governing the use of other people's material.

Plagiarism is when you copy or imitate another person's work and claim it as your own idea. The law of copyright protects work published by individuals or companies, whether in a website or in a book, magazine, etc. Breaking these laws is bad netiquette.

- Make sure you reference all items that are someone else's work. If you use any of the following, you must tell the reader where the work has come from:
  - words spoken by a person or ideas they have had
  - data that a person has collected
  - graphs, drawings or music created by someone else.

- Do not simply rearrange the words someone has already written.

- Use other people's web page designs as a source of ideas, not a template.

- Use pictures and quotes only where they add to your work.

If you wish to use an image, work or music from a website it is good netiquette to email the person who placed it on the WWW and ask if you can use the item.

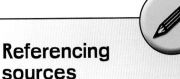

Referencing sources

1 Make a list of the different sources of information you might use in a project, e.g. books.

2 List the important information you need to record for each type of source, to avoid being accused of plagiarism. This is called referencing your sources. For example, for a web page you would record the URL.

3 If you are unsure whether you could use an image from a source on the Internet, how could you check?
   What things, other than images, might you need to obtain permission to use?

Searching the web

1 Search the web to find out:
   - How does a telephone work?
   - Who was King Darius?
   - Where can you buy books about fishing?
   - What is RAM?
   - Who is Bill Gates?

   Write down the URLs of the top five sites for each search.

2 Investigate each website you listed in question 1 and decide which category they are in:
   - Traditional references
   - Corporate
   - Individuals' sites
   - Governments and Universities

3 Write a short description of each site you listed in question 1.

4 Now find an online library.
   a How useful is this in confirming the information you have found in your searches?
   b Does the library provide useful links?

22 Creating a website

The WWW is made up of millions of websites. Some of these pages are created by professional designers, but most are made by individuals. To create websites you need to use Hyper Text Markup Language (HTML) – the instructions that form the basis of all websites.

Planning a website

Think of your website as a piece of advertising which must be planned and developed to capture the eye and imagination of the reader.

To build a good website you first need to decide on the topic, the purpose of the page and the audience the page is aimed at.

● *Topic*

If you are creating a website for a business, deciding on the topic of the page is not all that difficult. It is easy to see what a website for a school or book publishing company should be about. However, the purpose of these pages is not always clear.

● *Purpose*

The purpose of the page is very important. Is it to entertain, to advertise, to sell or to educate?

The table on the next page shows some of the key features of websites for different purposes.

Purpose	Key features of website
Education	• A theme • Fun approach • It should be easy to guess where links lead • Games • Clear information • Regularly updated
Sales	• The page must meet customer needs • Use of company colours, logos and designs • Clear links to the company's other websites • Should make good use of advertising opportunities • Should be easy for the customer to contact the company • Regularly updated
Entertainment	• Interactive • Access to video, audio or other site features should be rapid • Help pages • Regularly updated
Personal	• Unique presentation • Simple page design • Humour • Unique topic which captures the reader's imagination • Links to pages on similar topics • Regularly updated

● *Audience*

Knowing and understanding the audience for your website is the most important part of site planning. Readers should want to visit your site time after time. This means that your pages have to capture their imagination.

What does your audience want? This information can only be found through research.

Drafting the pages

Once you have decided on the topic and purpose of your website, you need to compile the text and graphics. Each item on every page should have a purpose and should add to the overall image of the site. What hyperlinks will you need to take your reader through the pages?

Collect all the site elements together. Then create a storyboard – a series of sketches to show what your pages will contain as you move through the hyperlinks between them. A storyboard helps you to get a feel for your creation.

Web pages can be a good way of keeping in touch with family and friends.

22

Website planning

Begin to plan your website here.

1 What is the topic of your website?

2 What is the purpose of your website?
   - educational   • sales
   - entertainment • personal

3 Who is your audience? Find out what they would like on the website.

4 What is the most important information your site will have on it?

5 What hyperlinks will your main page have? Where will these link to – other pages in your website, or other websites?

6 Create a storyboard for your website. Don't forget to include text.

7 Draw a site map showing how all your pages will link together – like this:

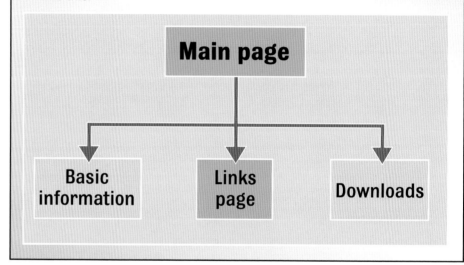

Creating the pages

The simplest way to begin to program in HTML is to use Windows® *Notepad* to type in the text and the HTML instructions.

- The HTML instructions (also known as 'tags') all have to be enclosed in <brackets>. Any text not in brackets will appear on screen.

- HTML instructions usually come in pairs around the text they affect. The second instruction starts with the / symbol, to show that this is the end of the instruction. For example:

  `<TITLE>This is the title</TITLE>`

- HTML documents always start with <HTML> and finish with </HTML>

- An HTML document is divided into two main sections – the <HEAD> and the <BODY>.

- The start or <HEAD> of any HTML document contains information about the page. The end of the <HEAD> section is shown by the instruction or tag </HEAD>

- The <BODY> section contains all the main instructions or code.

This example shows how to create a simple website with a title. The title is what your browser's caption bar will display when you view the page.

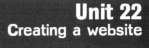

```
<HTML>
<HEAD>
<TITLE>My First Website</TITLE>
</HEAD>
<BODY>
Welcome to my first website.
</BODY>
</HTML>
```

Saving a web document

Save your work regularly as you create your pages.

Saving a web page

↗ Select **File**, **Save As**.

HTML files must always have the extension '.htm' so that the computer knows it should open them in a browser.

↗ Save your document as Page1.htm

Background colours

Change your body tag to:

```
<BODY BGCOLOR = "SILVER">
```

At the end of the body use the end tag </BODY> as before.

Notice you have to spell colour in the American way – color. If the instructions are not spelt correctly, the web browser will not recognise them.

This instruction gives a silver background to the website. There are other colours to choose from. Remember that the colour you choose should fit in with any theme or company colours you plan to use.

Black	Grey	White
Maroon	Navy	Blue
Green	Lime	Red
Teal	Yellow	Fuchsia
Aqua	Olive	Purple

Changing text size

Use the <FONT> instruction in the <BODY> section to change text size. Text in HTML has seven pre-set sizes, where 1 is the smallest and 7 the largest.

The commands:

```
<FONT SIZE = 7>Hello </FONT>
<FONT SIZE = 1>World</FONT>
```

would produce text in these sizes on a website:

Any text outside the <FONT> tags will revert to a pre-set size.

Here are some other instructions that you can use to alter the appearance of text.

<B>...</B>	**Bold**
<FONT COLOR = "RED"> ... </FONT>	Red text
<FONT FACE="ARIAL"> ... </FONT>	Use the Arial font
<I>...</I>	*Italic*
<U>...</U>	<u>Underlined</u>
<S> ... </S>	~~Strike~~
<TT> ... </TT>	M o n o s p a c e d
<BIG>...</BIG>	Text changed to a large font
<SMALL>...</SMALL>	Text changed to a small font
_{...}	Text appears as Subscript
^{...}	Text as appears as Superscript
 ...</BR>	Begins a new line

You can combine instructions like this:

```
<FONT FACE="ARIAL" SIZE=7 COLOR="FUCHSIA">Hello </FONT>
```

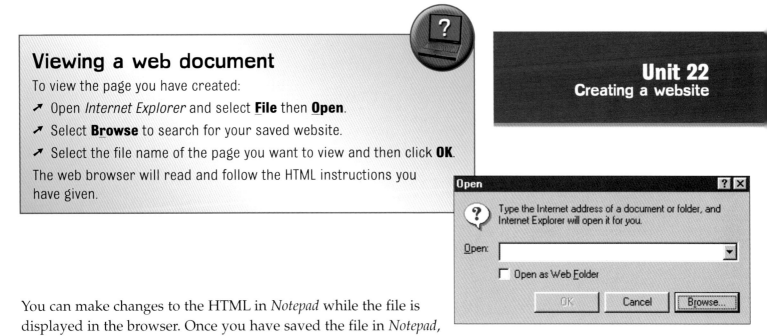

Viewing a web document

To view the page you have created:

↗ Open *Internet Explorer* and select **File** then **Open**.

↗ Select **Browse** to search for your saved website.

↗ Select the file name of the page you want to view and then click **OK**.

The web browser will read and follow the HTML instructions you have given.

You can make changes to the HTML in *Notepad* while the file is displayed in the browser. Once you have saved the file in *Notepad*, use the Refresh button to see the new version of the page.

Adding lines

Use horizontal lines to:

- Separate sections of text on different topics.
- Separate the title from the body of the page.

<HR>...</HR>   adds a horizontal line.

<HR Size = 6>   alters the line thickness. The larger the number, the thicker the line.

<HR Size=10 NoShade>   No shade makes the line solid. Otherwise the line has shading to make it appear 3D.

Adding images

Images can make a website stand out, but a website with a lot of images will load very slowly. As a rule, .gif or .jpg image files are smaller and allow high quality images to load quickly into a web browser.

Images should be:
- as small as possible
- included only if they are vital to the page
- avoided as a background for your website.

The tag to add an image to a website is:

<IMG SRC=" ">

Between the " " you need to type in the image's file name and directory path.

22

For example:

```
<IMG SRC="Hills.jpg">
```

```
<IMG SRC="D:/Pictures/Game/Hills.jpg">
```

The align command positions the image on the website.

```
<IMG SRC="MyImage.gif" ALIGN= RIGHT>
```

To add a background, rather than a foreground image use the format.

```
<BODY BACKGROUND ="MyImage.gif">
```

Linking pages

No website would be complete without links to other pages.

The tag to use is

```
<A HREF = "..."> ... </A>
```

Between the " " you can insert the file name of the page you wish to link to.

The hypertext link should appear underlined and blue.

Example webpage

These are the HTML instructions used to create the web page shown at the top of page 163.

```
<HTML>
<HEAD>
<TITLE>Tubby the Terrapin's first website</TITLE>
</HEAD>
<BODY BGCOLOR="SILVER">
<FONT SIZE=7> Hi I'm Tubby</FONT>
<HR Size=6></HR>
<BR>
<IMG SRC="Tubby.gif" ALIGN=LEFT>
<BR>
<BR>
<HR Size=6 NOSHADE></HR>
```

```
<FONT Size=1> My world</FONT>
can be lonely at times. Although I live with
Tessa, another terrapin
<BR>
I often find myself irritable and bad tempered.
Tessa avoids me when I am like this.
<BR>
<BR>
<BR>
<A HREF="Page2.htm">Click here to see a
picture of me.</A>
</BODY>
</HTML>
```

Hi I'm Tubby

My world can be lonely at times. Although I live with Tessa, another terrapin I often find myself irritable and bad tempered Tessa avoids me when I am like this.

Click here to see a picture of me.

Creating a local website

You are going to create a website about your town. It should include photographs and scanned drawings as well as text.

1 Search the web for sites about your town. Include suitable links on your website as further references.

2 Find one website from each category:

a a company website

b a school's website

c an individual's website

Write down the best and worst features of each site.

3 Find out what a midi file is. Then use the tag <BGSOUND="…"> to include background music for your website. Type the name of the midi file between the " ".

4 Experiment to find out what these tags do:

Tag 1
<UL>
<LI>company</LI>
<LI>school</LI>
<LI>individual</LI>
</UL>

Tag 2
<H1>Hi</H1>
<H6>Just passing through</H6>
<H3>Bye</H3>

Tag 3
<HR COLOR ="RED" NOSHADE></HR>
<Comment>What do I do?</Comment>

Planning a charity site

You have been asked to create a storyboard and site map for a charity that is involved in saving the Brazilian rainforests. The charity wishes to use the website to give up-to-date information on their campaign and the conditions in the rainforest.

1 Do some research on the Brazilian rainforest.

2 Design three different storyboards using the rainforest theme.

3 Take the best design and explain how you will:

- make the links clear to see

- show that the content of the site is accurate and unbiased.

4 Suggest a feature for the page that will attract interest from people who otherwise would not visit the charity's site.

23 Using email

Millions of people use email every day. It is good for business communication because it is quick and convenient. As more and more people own computers, more people use email for personal communication too.

In this unit you will:

• learn about the purpose of email

• discover the benefits of email

• learn about the features of email and email applications.

How email works

Email is short for Electronic Mail and it is a method of sending messages electronically by computer, using the Internet. It is an electronic postal service that doesn't need paper, envelopes or stamps.

Email is delivered seconds after it is sent, to anywhere in the world. This makes it the fastest available mail system, much quicker than the normal postal system, which is often called 'snail mail'.

Using email you can send simple text messages, or you can send computer programs, documents, pictures or sounds as **attachments** to an email.

To send or receive email you need:

• a PC with a modem so you can connect to the Internet via the telephone system

7 • an email account with an **Internet Service Provider (ISP)**

• an email application.

The ISP acts as a mailbox. Any email you send goes to your ISP mailbox and is then sent to its destination via the Internet. Email sent to you is held in the ISP mailbox until you decide to collect it.

7 The email gets to and from the ISP and the recipients over the Internet by a similar **route** to web pages requested by web browser.

Advantages and disadvantages of email

1 What are the disadvantages of email? How does snail mail (the postal service) have an advantage?

Would you use email or snail mail for these?

- A letter to a friend in America
- A birthday present
- A draft copy of a book or report
- A song you have recorded
- Photographs of a wedding, sent to a friend in Australia
- A computer operating system
- A song you have written (audio)
- A handwritten letter to a friend

2 Explain why email might be the best method in these situations.

- You have forgotten your Swiss friend's birthday.
- You have the only audio (sound) copy of your band's latest gig.
- You have the first draft of an article for a school newspaper and you want your friend to contribute to it.

Creating email messages

There are several different email applications, but most have the same types of features.

Address book

Some email applications have an address book that holds all the email addresses of your contacts – people you have sent email to. Instead of having to remember email addresses, you can browse through the address book and choose the correct address at the touch of a button. In Microsoft® *Outlook Express* selecting the 'To:' icon accesses the address book. In other applications there should be a clearly labelled button or menu for the address book.

When you add new contacts to your address book, most email applications allow you to enter personal details as well as the name and address. This can help you remember who the person is, as it is not always obvious from an email address.

23

Keep your address book up/to/date and delete contacts you no longer need, or it will become large and difficult to use.

With some email applications you can use your address book in other applications, such as mail merge and databases.

Header

The email header contains:

- The name and email address of the person you are sending the message to.
- The subject of the message.
- The name and email address of the person sending the message.

You can enter or edit these details by selecting the appropriate section of the header box on screen.

Remember that the address must be accurate. Even one letter wrong will mean that it cannot be delivered.

The person receiving your email will see the subject header before reading the message, so make sure it tells them clearly what the email is about.

Body

The body of the email is the message itself. This is usually text only, although it could include pictures. However not all email applications allow users to see graphics, so your message may not arrive looking as you intended it to. The safest way to send graphics is as an attachment (see next page).

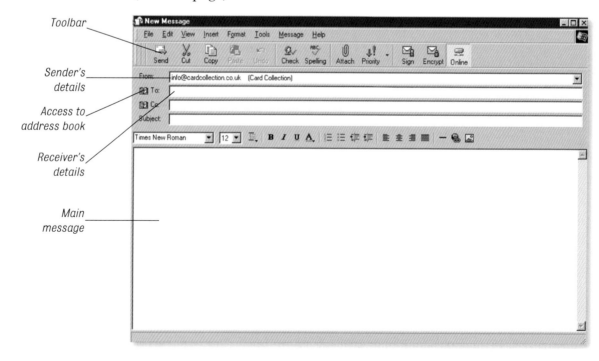

Toolbar

Sender's details

Access to address book

Receiver's details

Main message

Attachments

You can send documents, graphics and other types of files with your emails as attachments. All email applications allow you to attach files to your emails. There may be an attachments button, or a menu that allows you to insert attachments.

The person you send the attachment to needs to have the application that attachment was created in to be able to view it. If you used an unusual application to create the file, tell the recipient what it was, so they can acquire it to view your file.

Most email applications show when an email has an attachment, using an image such as a paperclip.

Send

Once your email is complete you need to send it. Your email application will have a Send button or menu option. Selecting this delivers your email to the ISP for the first part of its journey.

If you are not already connected to the Internet, selecting Send will usually prompt your computer to start connecting.

Encryption

Some applications have an encryption facility, which changes your email into a secret coded form so that others cannot read it. The person you send the email to will need an encryption key that you have provided for them, to decode your encrypted message.

Digital signature

Some email applications allow you to use a digital signature on your emails. A digital signature is a way of confirming who sent the email. It is evidence that the email comes from a genuine source.
A digital signature is useful if:
● an email is particularly important
● the reader is nervous about accepting email.

Email security

Email has one major drawback – it is not always secure. You can tell whether a letter has been opened before you receive it. But with an email you cannot be sure that it has not been read by someone else.

Email messages pass through several computers on their journey from sender to receiver. At each stage in this journey the email could be read, for example by someone working in the same company, a teacher, a hacker, a business competitor or a police officer. They will have their own reasons for accessing what you may think is confidential information.

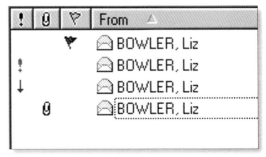

Email messages can be marked to show how important they are.

! *means urgent*

↓ *low priority*

❤ *already read and marked again for reading later*

You can use encryption to prevent others reading your email. The simplest way of protecting yourself from unwelcome readers is to treat each email as if it were a postcard that could be read by all. Do not use email for confidential or personal information.

The simple rule is that email messages should never contain information that is sensitive, offensive or illegal. The rules of netiquette (see page 154) apply to email just as they do on the Internet.

Remember! Anyone can read your emails.

Email ethics

1 What advice would you give to an employee or pupil who uses their work place or school to send personal emails?

2 Do you think it is right for an employee to use email at work for personal purposes?

3 Why might an employer wish to read employees' emails?

4 Do you think that employers, teachers or the police should have the power to reader other people's email?

List the 'for' and 'against' points in any argument you make.

Email addresses

All email addresses have the same basic format.

The company name or host name (account name).

The company that provides the email service.

The person's name.

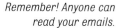
Name@hostname.freenetit.co.uk

The type of company providing the email service.

ac = academic (school, university)

gov = government office

co = company or business

org = organisation (charities)

The country where the email account is held.

Email addresses

1 Which countries do these email addresses come from?

.nz . uk .ca .de .ch

2 What type of organisations are the senders of these emails?

.mil .gov. .edu. .co. .org. .sch

3 Your friend has received an email from someone they met online. What advice would you give them about replying? Is there any information they should not give? Why?

Using email

1 Write an email to a person you have met online, telling them about yourself, hobbies, family, etc. Remember to follow the web wise netiquette rules on page 154.

2 Work in a group of 3 or 4. Collect a list of email contacts you have at home or school and enter these names into an address book.

3 Compose an email to some of your contacts, explaining that you are undertaking an email assignment at school. Ask them to reply with some details about themselves, their occupation and roughly where they live.

Get your teacher to check the email before you send it.

4 Put the information you received from question 3 on to a local, national or international map. Show your each contact's name, occupation and location.

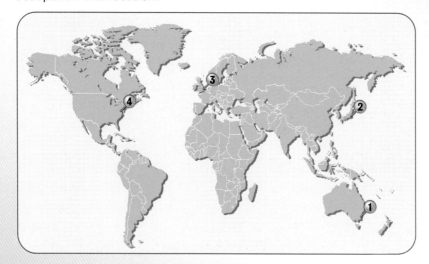

5 Did any of your contacts not follow the web wise rules? Why do you think this is?

Name: Gerry
Age: 13
Lives: Australia
Interests: Football and walking

Name: Tatsue
Age: 15
Lives: Japan
Interests: Computer games and aikido

Name: Rajesh
Age: 14
Lives: England
Interests: Music

Name: Bob and Julie
Age: 55 and 52
Lives: USA
Interests: Golf and cinema

Section B

Project 1

Connecting to the Internet

In this project you will:
- Create a display board showing how a user would connect to the Internet through an ISP and the hardware and software they would use.
- Write detailed descriptions of each stage of the connection process.
- Investigate some of the technical aspects of Internet connection.

Hardware and software

	Essential	Useful
Software	Internet browser DTP package	image manipulation package
Hardware	Internet connection	colour printer digital camera scanner

The project

Create a display board showing the different stages a computer user must go through to connect to the Internet through an ISP.

Work in a group of no more than four.

1 Write a description of each stage in the connection process (see the diagram on page 40).

2 Illustrate each stage with suitable graphics.

3 List all the components required to make this connection possible.

Key words and phrases for your Internet search are:
- How the Internet works
- Internet
- ISP

Project tasks

- Identify suitable websites and books to research Internet connection.
- Draw up a draft plan for your display, based on the resources you have found.
- Divide the different jobs between the members of your group.
- Set a time limit for completing each stage or task.

As you work on your project:

- Make good use of the notes or resources you have collected.
- Manipulate your images to show the areas you are interested in to best effect.
- Create and print draft versions of images and text. Suggest improvements you could make.
- Show your ideas to the class. Record any criticisms and make suitable changes.

When your project is completed:

- Present your work to your teacher. Explain the different stages of the connection process, including any additional information you have researched.
- Evaluate your work, using the prompts on page 190.

Section B

Project 2

Creating a resources database

In this project you will:
- Create a database of resources for a school department.
- Write a brief description of each resource.
- Ensure your database is easy to search for information.

Hardware and software:

	Essential	Useful

Software	Internet browser
	data-handling
	   program
	presentation package
		image manipulation
		   package

The project

Work in a group of no more than four.

Create a database of resources for a school subject that teachers and students can use for lessons or homework.

Your database should be divided into different topics within the subject. For example Modern Languages could include these topics:

- home
- school
- shopping.

For each topic identify relevant resources in the department and school library, such as worksheets, books, videos, Internet sites, activities, visits.

In your database record for each resource:

- name of the resource
- the type of resource (video, book, etc.)
- a brief description of the resource (approx 15 words)
- for books record the author
- for websites record any useful links

- topic(s) the resource can be used for
- where the resource is stored
- any other useful details.

Project tasks

- Find out about the different topics studied from the subject teacher.
- Identify suitable resources to be included for each topic.
- Create a field in your database where you can indicate how useful each resource is. Use headings such as: quality of information, quantity of information, number of topics covered, etc.
- Collect together all the details you need about each resource.
- Divide the different jobs between the members of your group.
- Set a time limit for completing each stage or task.

As you work on your project:

- Have regular meetings to discuss your progress with the database.
- Keep a master file of all the research you have done.
- Take minutes of all meetings. Type them up in a word processing package and save them in the master file.
- Create and print draft copies of your database.
- Show your database to the class. Record any criticisms and make suitable changes.

When your project is completed:

- Present your final product to a teacher in a presentation package.
- Test your database and record any comments.
- Evaluate your work using the prompts on page 190.

Internet search engines

In this project you will:

- Use Internet search engines and consider their features.
- Create a method of classifying each engine, and rate them according to a range of criteria.
- Create an information leaflet showing the advanced search rules for each different search engine.

Hardware and software

	Essential	Useful
Software	Internet browser spreadsheet package	presentation package DTP package
Hardware	stop watch	

The project

Create an information leaflet for an Internet Service Provider's customers, explaining the different advanced or complex searches available on search engines on the WWW.

Work in a group of no more than four.

For the leaflet you must rate each search engine's performance.

Test each search engine and rate them for:

- Finding suitable information. How many suitable sites does it find? How many of these sites are relevant to the search undertaken?
- How quickly does the engine access each site? Is this a valid measure?
- How effective are the browsing facilities?
- Layout
- Other

Project tasks

Before you begin work on your leaflet:

- Obtain a list from the Internet or your teacher of as many search engines as possible.
- Make a list of topics or words to use to test the engines.
- Use your chosen search words and undertake simple and complex searches on each engine.
- Record the minor differences in the way complex searches are done on each engine.
- Record the time taken to display the first page of results.
- Record the number of sites the engine finds for each search.
- Graph your results for the speed of each engine and number of sites found.
- Record your observations about each site's layout and any other criteria.

As you are creating your leaflet:

- Make good use notes of the notes you have made.
- Use screen dumps to illustrate key points.
- Show the ratings for each engine under the criteria you have observed.
- Create and print draft versions of images and text. Suggest improvements you could make.
- Show your ideas to the class. Record any criticisms and make suitable changes.

When your project is completed:

- Present your leaflet to your teacher.
- Evaluate your work using the prompts on page 190.

National Curriculum projects

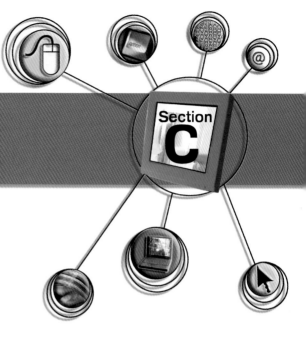

These projects give you a chance to use your ICT skills. They also help you to see when and how ICT can be useful.

Section C

Project 1

All about me

In this project you will:
- Use a presentation package to make a presentation about yourself.
- Use a scanner and digital camera to bring digital images into a presentation.

Hardware and software

	Essential	Useful
Software	presentation package	image manipulation package
Hardware	digital camera scanner	

The project

Produce a presentation about yourself to tell others about:
- your family
- your hobbies and interests
- your likes and dislikes, strengths and weaknesses
- your future plans – career, etc.
- your feelings on your first day at school
- what you felt like on the first day of secondary school.

Your presentation should have up to five slides and should include images.

Project tasks

- Decide what information you will include in your presentation.
- Storyboard your ideas.
- Make a list of the images you will use and where they will come from.
- Note on your list if images require scanning, cropping or editing before use.
- Experiment with your presentation package to make sure you understand all its features.

As you work on your project:

- Have a group 'brainstorming' session for ideas before you start work on your own presentation.
- Storyboard each slide for your presentation, giving details about:
  - The main theme for each slide.
  - The size and type of font for titles and main text.
  - Ideas for pictures to include and possible sources for these.
  - Ideas for sound effects or background music, and possible sources.
- Show your ideas to a friend. Write down any suggestions they make.
- Make any necessary changes to your storyboards, taking account of your friend's suggestions.
- As you work on your slides, make good use of your notes and resources you have collected.
- Create and print draft copies of your presentation, commenting upon changes that you could make to improve its appearance.
- Show your presentation to the class. Record any criticisms and make suitable changes.

When your project is completed:

- Show your presentation to your teacher or your class.
- Evaulate your work using the prompts on page 190.

Section C

Project 2

Collecting information and presenting ideas

In this project you will:
- Collect images from a number of different sources to make a presentation.
- Select suitable images for your purpose and audience.
- Edit your images.
- Present your images in a presentation.

Hardware and software

	Essential	Useful
Software	presentation package *ClipArt* image manipulation package	web browser images on CD rom drawing package
Hardware	scanner	digital camera

The project

Work in a group of no more than four.

Prepare a presentation for an assembly on a theme of your choice. Your presentation should have up to 12 slides.

Here are a few suggestions for themes:

- A school issue such as litter, vandalism or school lunches.
- An issue in the local community, e.g. the proposed closure of the cottage hospital or the campaign for a zebra crossing outside the primary school.
- A local charity.
- A national charity, such as the Royal National Lifeboat Institute or the People's Dispensary for Sick Animals.
- An international charity or cause, such as Third World Debt, Christian Aid, global warming.

- An issue in the national or international news, such as the possible closure of a large car manufacturing company close to the school.

Project tasks

Choose a topic.

- Have a short 'brainstorming' session on how to present the topic. Select the best approach.
- Storyboard your ideas.
- Decide on the images for each slide and where you will find them. Remember that the images should be appropriate for your audience.
- Decide who will look for each image.

As you work on your project:

- Collect the images you need. Use the library, scanned images, digital images, *ClipArt* from the Internet or CD-rom, images from the Internet (check copyright restrictions), your own drawings or photographs.
- Edit your images in a suitable program.
- Use cropping, recolouring and resizing.
- Write out your script or prompts.
- Decide who will say what.
- Practise your presentation.
- Show your presentation to the class. Record any criticisms and make suitable changes.

When your project is completed:

- Show your presentation to your teacher or your class.
- Evaluate your work using the prompts on page 190.

Section C

Project 3

Delivering the news

In this project you will:

- Produce a newsletter for new students at your school.
- Produce a similar newsletter for parents, giving key information about the school.
- Develop your newsletter so that it can be used as a 'template' for future editions.

Hardware and software

	Essential	Useful
Software	DTP or word processing package *ClipArt*	image manipulation package
Hardware	digital camera	colour printer scanner

The project

Work in a group of no more than four.

Create a two-page newsletter for new year 7 pupils coming into your school, telling them everything they need to know before they start.

Create a similar newsletter for these pupils' parents, telling them about the school their son or daughter will attend.

Ensure that both newsletters are suitable for their intended audiences.

Project tasks

For the pupils' newsletter:

Make a list of everything you think a new pupil would need to know about your school.

- What sort of information were you given when you moved up from primary school?
- What sort of things did you want to know?

Here are some suggestions:

- How to find your way around the school.
- Who to ask if you needed something.
- Where you could go at lunchtime, and which areas were out of bounds.
- What clubs there are.
- Who could help you with your school work.
- What sporting activities are available.

From this list decide what information you need to find from other people.

- How will you make the newsletter interesting?
- Do you need cartoons or photographs?
- Once you have decided on the information and images to include, sketch out the layout of your newsletter.

For the parents' newsletter:

This newsletter should be up to two pages long.

- What will be the main differences between this newsletter and the one for pupils?
- How will you distribute it? Remember the pupils are not at the school yet.
- What will parents want to know about their child's new school?
- Will they need more or less information about holidays, contact names and numbers? What sort of information does the school require from parents? Should there be a form for them to return, giving this information?
- Once you have decided on the information and images to include, sketch out the layout of your newsletter.

As you work on your project:

- Find the images you need. Use a digital camera to take photographs around the school.
- Divide up the tasks between you, so you each work on different articles.
- Edit your images in a suitable package
- Show the pupils' newsletter to a year 7 class. Show the parents' newsletter to parents of children at the school. Record any criticisms and make changes.

When your project is completed:

- Present your newsletters to your teacher or your class.
- Evaluate your work using the prompts on page 190.

Section C

Project 4

Healthy eating

In this project you will:

- Use formulas to create a spreadsheet calculator that works out calorie intake levels.
- Produce a graph or chart of ideal body weights.
- Produce a leaflet about healthy eating.

Hardware and software

	Essential	Useful
Software	DTP package spreadsheet web browser	image manipulation package
Hardware		colour printer

The project

For a health centre, create:

- a calorie calculator spreadsheet
- a graph or chart for calculating ideal body weight for different individuals
- a leaflet that gives advice about healthy eating.

Project tasks

This project is for individual work.

Research healthy eating on the Internet. Use information from these websites:

- www.nal.usda.gov/fnic/foodcomp
- www.mcdonalds.com
- www.caloriecontrol.org
- www.healthyeating.org

Find other websites using these key words:

- healthy living
- body mass index
- calories
- food tables

Work out the required calorie intake for different types of people, e.g. adult male, adult female, child, older person, etc.

- Set up a spreadsheet to record information about:
  - Typical daily calorie needs for males and females.
  - Typical calories burnt up by different types of exercise.
  - Calorie intake for individual people.
- Use your spreadsheet to calculate from this information whether an individual is eating too many or too few calories per day.
- Make a suggestion about how they could change their routine or diet to ensure weight loss, weight gain or a stable weight.

As you work on your project:

- Keep a master file of your research.
- Create and print draft copies of your spreadsheet, chart and leaflet.
- Try out your spreadsheet, chart and leaflet on your class. Record any criticisms and make suitable changes.

When your project is completed:

- Show your presentation to your teacher or your class.
- Evaluate your work using the prompts on page 190.

Section C

Project 5

Questionnaire

In this project you will:
- Create a questionnaire to find out where litter is a problem in your school.
- Record your results in a database.
- Investigate the areas identified by your questionnaire.
- Graph the results of your investigation.
- Produce a report, including suggestions for tackling the litter problem.

Hardware and software

	Essential	Useful
Software	database package DTP or word processing package	
Hardware	digital camera	colour printer scanner

The project

Work in a group of no more than four.

Create a questionnaire to find out whether pupils think the school has a litter problem, where the problem is most serious, and how it could be prevented.

- Get 15 pupils to complete your questionnaire.
- Record their answers in a database.
- Count the items of litter in the litter problem areas pupils identify. Use a quadrat to mark off a one-metre square in each area and count the pieces of litter within it to get a value for pieces of litter per square metre.
- Record the results in a spreadsheet and graph the results.
- Compare the pupil questionnaires with your results. Did the students identify the worst litter areas?
- Make a display of your findings. Include suggestions for how the litter problem could be reduced.

Project tasks

- Identify suitable questions for your questionnaire.
- Refine these questions.
- Print the questionnaire and get students to complete it.
- Divide the different jobs between the members of your group.
- Enter the results of your questionnaire in a database. Ensure that your database uses validation techniques to reduce errors.
- Use queries and filters to draw out important statistics about your school.

As you work on your project:

- Make a map showing the areas students identify as litter-free and full of litter.
- Find or produce suitable images for your display.
- Produce graphs and charts of your questionnaire results and litter counting results.
- Comment on anything that may have affected your results.
- Discuss reasons why particular areas have more litter than others.
- Discuss ways of reducing the amount of litter.
- Show a draft version of your display to the class. Record any criticisms and make suitable changes.

When your project is completed:

- Show your presentation to your teacher or your class.
- Evaluate your work using the prompts on page 190.

Section C

Project 6

Control sequences

In this project you will:
- Write a control sequence.
- Develop flowcharts for a control sequence.
- Use inputs in your control sequence.

Hardware and software

	Essential	Useful
Software	control software	

Hardware	control box/
	  interface device
	input and
	  output devices
		colour printer
		scanner

The project

Design a control sequence that operates an automatic door into a supermarket.

Important information:

1. The door is operated by a key pad. When four keys are pressed in the correct sequence, the door will unlock and remain open for 10 seconds and then close again.

2. The door remains closed until there is an input, either from a pressure sensitive pad or from a light gate. The door then opens and closes 10 seconds later.

3. Further inputs from the pressure pad or light gate will open the door again. It closes 10 seconds later.

4. The door can be locked by re-entering the key pad code or your own choice of input.

5. The system uses limit switches to sense when the door is fully open and fully closed. The motor is halted in response to the feedback from these microswitches.

Project tasks

- Draw your flowchart showing the circuit required for the door.
- If you have control software, recreate your circuit on a computer.
- Experiment with different lengths of time for the doors to stay open.
- Modify the system so that the doors open automatically on input from a light gate.
- Find another suitable input to detect when the doors can safely be closed, rather than waiting for 10 seconds. This input must detect that the person has gone through the door and that there is no-one else about to go through the door from the other side.

As you work on your project:

Produce a report on your project, including:

- a description of how your automatic door will work.
- the software and hardware components of your control system.
- flowcharts of your control sequences.
- the input and output devices that you use.
- the flowchart you have designed to control outputs.
- Show what tests you have undertaken to see if your flowchart works.
- Show your flowchart to the class. Record any criticisms and make suitable changes.

When your project is completed:

- Show your flowchart to your teacher or your class.
- Evaluate your work using the prompts on page 190.

Section C

Vital statistics

In this project you will:

- Collect statistics that change over time.
- Check the accuracy of the information.
- Use a data handling program to analyse and chart the information.

Hardware and software

	Essential	Useful
Software	spreadsheet package	web browser
		CD-rom reference e.g. *Social Trends, Europe in the Round*
		newspapers
		Ceefax

The project

This project is for individual work.

Choose some data that interests you. Monitor, record and present data values as they change over a given time period.

Your data may come from a primary source (from first-hand observations, e.g. daily temperatures) or from a secondary source (already recorded, e.g. average income per household over a given period).

Here are a few ideas:

- The weather in your home town and the weather in your twinned town, using daily or monthly figures.
- The value of shares in a local company every working day for at least one month.
- The value of the pound (£) against the dollar ($) or the euro (€) for one month.
- The number of people visiting a local attraction during a month.

Weather statistics can be found on www.met-office.gov.uk

Share prices can be found on Ceefax or on www.yahoo.co.uk

Project tasks

- When you have decided upon your topic, think about all the different sources of information you could use.
- For each source write down all the strengths and weaknesses.
- Only use information that you can prove is current or up to date.
- Decide on at least two different sources to use. This allows you to check the accuracy of the data.

As you work on your project:

- Write an introduction explaining what information you are using and what you think you might discover or prove, e.g.
    - When it rains people visit local attractions less.
    - That the weather in your town and twinned town is always similar.
- Keep regular records of your data in a suitable software package.
- Experiment with different ways of charting your data. Choose a chart that displays your data effectively.
- Produce a chart of your data with a written report on the results of your investigation.
- Show your charts and report to the class. Record any criticisms and make suitable changes.
- Look back at what you have discovered. Was it what you expected?

When your project is completed:

- Show your charts and report to your teacher or your class.
- Evaluate your work using the prompts on page 190.

Section C

Project 8

Creating council websites

In this project you will:

- Create two websites using HTML.
- Link your websites to each other and to other suitable sites.
- Evaluate each site you link to for its overall quality, and its usefulness as a link to your site.
- Create a presentation or display to show the features of your sites.

Hardware and software

	Essential	Useful

Software	Internet browser
	Notepad
		presentation
		  package
		word processing
		  package

The project

Create two websites for the local council. Each website should have 3–5 pages and should link to the local council website.

1 A website for tourists who wish to find out about the area before they visit.

2 A website for local people with pages on local history, popular places to visit, etc. and links to websites for the local radio stations, newspapers, shops and schools.

Your two sites should link to each other in a useful way.

Try these websites for ideas or information to get you started:

www.multimap.com

www.RAC.co.uk

www.theaa.co.uk

www.touristinformation.co.uk

Key words and phrases for your Internet search are:

Local government

"UK radio stations"

"Places to visit in the UK"

Project tasks

- Create a storyboard showing how the web pages will look.
- Create a site map showing how the pages will link together and to other websites.
- Write a detailed evaluation of each site you are going to link to, explaining how it will be useful for the users of your site. Include these evaluations on your website to help visitors decide where to link to.

As you work on your project:

- Create your web pages in HTML.
- Keep a record of websites you have collected information from and the source and copyright details of any images you use. Credit the image sources on your web pages.
- Create a presentation or a display to launch your finished site to the council. Include screen shots of your websites in the presentation.
- Show your presentation to the class. Record any criticisms and make suitable changes.

When your project is completed:

- Show your presentation to your teacher or your class.
- Evaluate your work using the prompts on page 190.

Section C

Project 9

Creating a personal website

In this project you will:

- Research and plan a website on a topic of your choice.
- Create your website using HTML.
- Make your site a reliable source of information, by including useful links and referencing sources.

Hardware and software

	Essential	Useful
Software	Internet browser *Notepad*	image manipulation package
Hardware		digital camera scanner

The project

Create a website on a topic of your choice. The website should be an introduction to this topic for other Internet users.

Your website should have up to 5 pages.

Project tasks

- Choose your topic.
- List all the resources you can use, e.g. books, images, other Internet sites.
- Make a list of useful websites you could link to. What will each of these links add to your website? Do they provide:
  - supporting information
  - a different viewpoint
  - links for further research
  - any other features?
- Are the sites you will link to reliable sources of information? Explain your reasoning.
- Create a storyboard showing how the web pages will look.

- Create a site map showing how the pages link together and to other websites.

As you work on your project:

- Use the resources you have collected.
- Identify ways that you can make your website a reliable information source.
- Make a rough draft of each page. For each page indicate:
  - the main purpose of the page
  - the size and type of font you will use for main text and headings
  - notes on the images you would like to use
  - ideas for sound effects and background music.
- Obtain or create suitable images to use in your website.
- Reference any images you use from other websites and provide links to these sites.
- Print copies of your web pages and show them to the class. Record any criticisms and make suitable changes.

When your project is completed:

- Show your website pages to your teacher or your class.
- Evaluate your work using the prompts on page 190.

Section C

Project 10

Debating an issue

In this project you will:
- Prepare arguments either 'for' or 'against' a motion in a debate, supported by references and images.
- Search the WWW for information on your chosen issue.
- Evaluate and reference your information so it is convincing to use in a debate.

Hardware and software

	Essential	Useful
Software	web browser word processing package	presentation package DTP package encyclopaedia or topic-based CD-roms
Hardware		scanner

The project

Work in a group of four. Split into two pairs. One pair should investigate the 'for' arguments and the other group the 'against' arguments for one of these motions:

1 Fox hunting should be banned.

2 Hacking is harmless fun for computer enthusiasts.

3 Genetically modified foods are a great benefit to society.

4 Scientists should develop cloning techniques.

Each pair should make a presentation of the top three arguments.

Debate the motion you have chosen.

Some sites that may be useful:

www.rspca.org.uk

www.foe.co.uk

www.zinezone.com

www.greenpeace.org.uk

www.newscientist.com

Key words and phrases for your Internet search:

Virus	Hacker
Cloning	Genetic developments
Deforestation	"Save the whale"
Hunting	

Project tasks

- List the websites you used to find information.
- Evaluate the websites you used and list them in order, starting with the most reliable source.
- Use information from the top three sites on the list to prepare three arguments 'for' or 'against' the issue. You could email the author of the website to find out more about the topic.
- Create a presentation of your three arguments. State and explain your three arguments briefly and clearly. Use pictures and site references to support your statements and to demonstrate the reliability of your source.

As you work on your project:

- Try to guess the arguments your opponents will use and prepare counter arguments to prove them wrong. Collect images and references that could disprove or question the validity of their arguments.
- Use your presentation in a debate in front of the class. The pairs should take turns to present a single argument and allow the other pair time to present a counter argument.

After the debate:

- Evaluate your work using the prompts on page 190.

Section C

Project 11

Using data

In this project you will:

- Use the Internet to research bar codes and scanning.
- Investigate how shops collect data using EPOS (electronic point of sale) and loyalty cards.
- Use bar codes to identify products and build a profile of the customer who buys them.

Hardware and software

	Essential	Useful
Software	web browser wordprocessing or DTP package	*ClipArt*
Hardware		colour printer scanner

The project

Work in a group of no more than four.

Create a display showing how supermarkets collect and use data on their customers.

Project tasks

Task 1

- On the Internet research bar codes and scanning (see Unit 3). Useful websites include www.deBarcode.com and www.BarCode1.com

Task 2

- See Unit 6, for information on EPOS and loyalty cards. How do supermarkets use these to collect data? www.howstuffworks.com is a useful website for this research.
- Produce a chart showing the advantages and disadvantages of a supermarket loyalty card to both customers and retailers.

Task 3

- Collect supermarket till receipts for a display, labelling the different items printed on them. What data does the supermarket store on each transaction?
- Identify the products from the barcodes in the table below, using www.deBarcode.com and www.BarCode1.com or any other suitable website.

Bar code	Product
50 25232 05131 1	
4 902580 320782	
0 23272 11063 5	
5 013738 656154	
5 025966 246588	
0 28946 05972 2	

- All these products were part of one customer's weekly shop. Write a customer profile for this customer, based on what you know about the products he or she buys.

Customer profile	
Female:	Age 35–45
Parent:	Children in age range 2–12 years
Pets:	dog, cat
Special interests:	organic foods, multipacks, fresh fruit, cheeses
Shops:	weekly

- What types of special offers may this customer be interested in?

As you work on your project:

- Divide the different jobs between the members of your group.
- Set a time limit for completing each task.
- Keep a master file of all the research you do.
- Record the details of useful websites you use.

When your project is completed:

- Show your project to your teacher or your class.
- Evaluate your work using the prompts on page 190.

Section C

Project 12

Planning a fund-raising event

In this project you will:

- Plan and prepare a fund-raising event.
- Decide who you need to contact and the best way of contacting them. Prepare a mail merge letter.
- Produce advertising for the event.
- Create a spreadsheet to forecast the amount of money raised.

Hardware and software

	Essential	Useful

Software	mail merge
	DTP package
	word processing
	  package
	spreadsheet
	  package
		ClipArt

Hardware		colour printer scanner

The project

Work in a group of no more than four.

Plan a fund-raising event for a local or national charity.

Project tasks

- Choose a charity to support.
- Decide on a suitable event, e.g. a fete, a sale, an evening event, a carnival. Fix a date and time.
- Make a list of the attractions at the event, e.g. food, entertainment, live band, disco, amusements, personalities, well-known racing cars, memorabilia from a famous person, special features such as helicopter rides, etc.
- Decide who needs to be involved in the planning, the organisation and the event itself.
- Draw up an action plan for the event. Include dates when each action needs to be completed. Calculate the dates by working back from the planned event day.

- Create the advertising for the event.
- Set up a spreadsheet to forecast the profit for the event.

Task 1

- Make a list of the attractions of the event, then decide on the resources you need.
- List the people to contact to obtain the resources you need. For each person on the list decide on the best method of contacting them, e.g. letter, telephone, email.
- Suggest suitable sources for the addresses and phone numbers of companies and agencies you need to contact.
- Prepare a letter that you can mail merge to send to people on your contact list.
  - Design the letterhead for your letters.
  - Lay out your document in a suitable style. Introductions and general information can be written in paragraphs but specific requests should be in bulleted lists.
  - Ask if discounts are available, as this is a charity event.
  - Ask each stall holder, attraction, etc. for a donation to the charity.
  - Include the dates when you need things, and request that they send you confirmation of what they can provide.

Task 2

- Decide on the best way of attracting the people that you want to attend the event, e.g. posters to be put up around the town, advertisements for newspapers, a website or advertisement you can email to people.

- Create your advertising materials. Make it clear that the event is to raise money for your charity. Ensure that the style is suitable for where the advertising will be used.

Task 3

- Produce a programme for the event, which can be sold either on the door or in advance.
- Include a map of how to get there and a plan of the site showing where different attractions will be.
- Include a timetable for the event.

Task 4

- The purpose of the event is to raise money. Create a spreadsheet that allows you to project how much you expect to raise and how much you will have to spend, for different numbers of people attending.
- Under costs include:
  - Hire of the venue, facilities such as toilets, food providers, fencing for car parks, stalls, etc.
  - Staff, e.g. cleaners, car park attendants.
  - Publicity materials and advertising costs.
  - Special attractions.
- Under income include:
  - A donation from each stall holder or attraction.
  - Entry fees.

As you work on your project:

- Brainstorm your ideas before you start.
- Draft your ideas for your:
  - posters
  - advertising leaflets
  - letterhead
  - spreadsheet, showing all the formulae
  - signs for each stallholder, keeping to a standard design.
  - map
  - event programme

- Draft a document setting out the style for all the materials you produce. Consider, e.g.
  - Will you have a slogan or logo?
  - Will your logo always be in a certain position, or a certain size?
  - Will you always use the same fonts for posters, etc? This will make the event look more professional.
  - When will you show contact names, numbers and addresses? When will these be left off?
  - Which pieces of information must be included in every document? e.g. date, time, place?
- On each draft document, highlight:
  - The main purpose of the document.
  - Ideas of pictures to include.
  - The type size and style for main headings and body text.
  - The features standard to all your documents, from the standards list above.
- Discuss your ideas with the group. Write down any suggestions they make.
- Make any changes necessary as a result of these suggestions.
- Divide the different jobs between the members of your group.
- Set a time limit for completing each task.
- Keep a master file of all the research you do.
- Show your plans, with all the materials you have produced, to the class. Record any criticisms and make suitable changes.

When your project is completed:

- Present your plan for the event and all the materials you have produced to your teacher or your class.
- As a group, make a list of all the things that did not go according to plan. Explain why this happened and any lessons you can learn from this.
- As a group, make a list of the things that went well.
- Evaluate your work using the prompts on page 190.

Section C

Project 13

Control sequences

In this project you will:

- Develop procedures into a control sequence.
- Use multiple inputs to your control sequence.
- Provide feedback to monitor your control sequence.
- Control different types of output systems.

Hardware and software

	Essential	Useful
Software	control package presentation package	
Hardware	control box/ interface device input and output devices	wireless remote-controlled vehicles and robots infra-red link hardware

The project

Design a system that will prevent two trains on the same track getting closer together than a prescribed distance. You should be able to use your system, with slight modifications, for road transport, e.g. buses and lorries.

Project tasks

- Decide on the inputs from the vehicles. Investigate 'gates' set at regular intervals along the track or road using infra-red links, or simpler light gates.

These inputs need to give information on the position of the vehicle to a system which then carries out further 'condition dependent' commands, e.g. stopping, slowing down or speeding up.

- When you have data about one vehicle's position you can measure the distance between two or more vehicles, either travelling in the same direction, or different directions.

- Use variables within the system to keep each vehicle a set distance apart.
- Incorporate a warning light to indicate when two or more vehicles are too close together, to warn the driver that he or she may have to make adjustments.
- Produce a system that stops vehicles or modifies their speed automatically under certain circumstances.

You may be able to combine this work with an electronics project in Design and Technology.

As you work on your project:

- Produce notes describing your system and how it works. Where could this control system be used in the real world? Why would it be useful?
- Produce notes on the software and hardware components of this control system, including images of your system.
- Produce a flowchart to show your control sequences. Describe the input and output devices that you use and why wireless systems are best in this situation.
- In your flowchart, describe how parts of your sequence use feedback loops. Identify and describe the sections that use open and closed loop control.
- Show your notes and images to the class. Record any criticisms and make suitable changes.

When your project is completed:

- Show your notes and images to your teacher or your class.
- Evaluate your work using the prompts on page 190.

Section C

Project 14

Email

In this project you will:
- Use email to communicate with your working partner.
- Create documents and attach these to emails.

Hardware and software

	Essential	Useful
Software	email package that supports attachments word processing package	DTP package image manipulation package

The project

Work in pairs. You may only communicate with your partner by email.

Create four information sheets for first-time users of your wordprocessing package.

There should be one information sheet for each of these topics:

- Enter text and change the font size and style.
- Use the spell check facility.
- Move the text to the right, centre or left of the page.
- Add bullet points.

The information sheets should include screen dumps which have been edited in an image manipulation package, as well as text instructions.

Project tasks

- Before you start work, share your ideas for the project by email. Add to each other's lists of ideas until you both have one comprehensive list.

- Draft your ideas for your information sheets and comment on the ideas by email. Agree on:
  - Layout for each sheet.
  - Fonts and font sizes to use.
  - The package you will use to create the documents.
  - Will you have a slogan or logo on your sheets?
  - What pieces of information should go on each sheet, e.g websites for further help in using *Word*, contact names and email addresses?

- By email, decide with your partner which two sheets you will each write.

- On each draft document highlight:
  - The main purpose of the document.
  - Ideas of pictures to include, and sources.
  - Items standard to all your documents.

- Respond to all your partner's suggestions by email, explaining whether you think they are good or poor. Remember to be positive, always suggesting improvements and praising good work.

As you work on your project:

- Send your ideas and drafts of your information sheets to each other by email, as attachments.

- Use the comment or note facilities in your word processing package to comment on each other's ideas and suggest improvements and corrections.

When your project is completed:

- Show your information sheets to your teacher or your class.
- Evaluate your work using the prompts on page 190.

Section C

Project 15

Enterprise model

In this project you will:
- Create a spreadsheet to model the working of a mini-enterprise.
- Run test data in the model.

Hardware and software

	Essential	Useful
Software	spreadsheet package DTP package	web browser image manipulation package *ClipArt*
Hardware		colour printer

The project

Work in a group of no more than four.

- Use a spreadsheet to model the costs and profits for a mini-enterprise in school.
- Use a database to record information collected from potential customers about the products or services they would like you to offer.
- Use a word processing package to create posters, tickets, etc.

The type of mini-enterprise is not important, as you do not really have to run it.

Here are a few ideas:

- Selling individually designed greeting cards.
- Raising money for charity through an inter-tutor group fancy dress basketball competition. Teams pay to enter and staff and students from other year groups pay to watch. Prizes sponsored by local businesses, certificates made in a DTP package.
- School disco to raise funds for a school minibus.
- Raising money for charity through washing cars.
- Selling refreshments at a school production to raise money to cover production costs.

Project tasks

- Have a group 'brainstorming' session on mini-enterprise ideas and then select one.
- Divide up the tasks between the group. Separate the tasks using spreadsheets, word processing, DTP and graphics packages and assign appropriate desk tasks to each person.
- List the types of costs and income for your enterprise.
- Plan your spreadsheet model.
  - What calculations will you need to make?
  - What costs and prices will you need to predict?
  - Which formulae will you use?
  - What data will you need to collect in advance?
- Design your spreadsheet model.
  - Who will use your model?
  - What functions will the user need to make best use of this model e.g. queries in a database, mail merge in a word processing package, etc?
- Run your model using test data.
  - Test that your model works by comparing the answers it gives with a set of answers calculated by hand.
  - Test each section of your model a few times.
  - Print out the evidence that your spreadsheet works.
  - If you have used mail merge or other activities, test these too.

As you work on your project:

- Divide the different jobs between the members of your group.
- Set a time limit for completing each task.
- Show draft documents, etc. to the class. Record any criticisms and make suitable changes.

When your project is completed:

- Present everything you have produced to your teacher.
- Evaluate your work using the prompts on page 190.

Project evaluation

It is important to evaluate your project work after you have completed it. By looking critically at your work, you can identify how you can improve your ways of working and using ICT, as well as the final product.

Use the following prompts to evaluate your project.

Looking back at planning

- List the things you aimed to achieve when you started the project.
- Have you achieved them all?
- If not, what stopped you achieving them?
- Have you achieved any additional things that you had not planned to?

Hardware and software

- List the software and hardware you used in your project. Explain what you used each for.
- How easy/difficult did you find it to use each piece of software and hardware?
- Did you have any problems with the hardware? Describe any problems you had and say why you think they occurred. What could you do in future to avoid these problems?
- Would it have been better to have used different hardware or software in the project?
- Do you have equipment or software at home that would have been easier to use? Explain your answer.

Control software

- Did your control system work?
- What changes did you make to your control sequence to make it work smoothly?
- Why did you make these changes?

Audience

- Who was your audience?
- For what parts of your project did you have to consider the audience?
- How did you think your audience would react to your work?
- How did your audience react to your work?

- What improvements did your audience suggest?
- How could you have improved your work?

General

- What did you think of your project overall?
- What problems did you have while working on this project?
- How did you overcome these problems?
- Give yourself marks out of 5 for each aspect of your project work in this table

Aspect of project work	Mark
Planning Amount of planning you did Overall plan for project followed Project handed in on time	
Presentation Layout Ease of reading Use of graphics Use of white space Choice of font style and size	
Usefulness How easy is it to use? How easy is the design to understand and amend? How suitable is it for its intended audience and purpose?	
Quality of research Amount of research Number of different research sources Quality of research sites and materials used	
General Final presentation of the project – bound, stapled, loose leaf, etc. Time spent on evaluation task Effort put into this project	

Which areas do you need to improve most?

- Do you think you put enough effort into this project?
- What is the main aspect you would like to improve in your next project?

Glossary/Index